FAILURE OF A REVOLUTION
Germany 1918–19

Sebastian Haffner

FAILURE OF
A REVOLUTION

Germany 1918–19

Translated by Georg Rapp

THE LIBRARY PRESS

Distributed by
OPEN COURT
Publishing Co.
La Salle, Ill. 61301

800-435-6850   or   815-223-2521

First published in the United States in 1973 by
The Library Press

Copyright © 1969 by Scherz Verlag
Berne, Munich, Vienna
Translation copyright © 1973 by
André Deutsch Limited
All rights reserved

First published in Germany under
the title *Die Verratene Revolution* by
Scherz Verlag

Printed in Great Britain

Library of Congress Catalog Card Number: 72-373

International Standard Book Number: 0-912050-23-3

And let me speak to th'yet unknowing world
How these things came about; so shall you hear
Of carnal, bloody and unnatural acts,
Of accidental judgements, casual slaughters,
Of deaths put on by cunning and forced cause,
And, in this upshot, purposes mistook
Fall'n on th'inventors' heads: all this can I
Truly deliver.

SHAKESPEARE – *Hamlet 5, ii*

Contents

List of Illustrations

Preface

Franz Kafka's story *Before the Law* is of a man at a gate demanding entry. Invariably repulsed by the gatekeeper he spends his entire life waiting expectantly outside the gate where he vainly keeps trying to persuade him to relent. Finally, in the hour of his death, as his hearing begins to fail, the gatekeeper roars into his ear: 'No one else could ever be admitted here since this gate was made only for you. I am now going to shut it.'

One is reminded of this Kafka story in musing over the history of the German Empire and of German Social Democracy. Created almost simultaneously, they seemed meant for each other: Bismarck had put together the outer framework of state within which Social Democracy was able to spread its wings and which it hoped one day to fill with lasting and significant political substance. If this hope had come true – perhaps the German Empire would still be in existence.

As is well known, it did not come true. The German Empire fell into the wrong hands and went under. In the seventy-four years of its existence Social Democracy, which from the beginning had felt called upon to lead the Empire and might have saved it, never found the courage and strength to grasp power. Like the man in Kafka's story, Social Democracy had made its bed outside the gate. And in 1945 world history might have roared into its ears: 'This gate was made only for you. I am now going to shut it.'

But unlike Kafka's tale, this story has a dramatic moment when everything seemed about to change. Faced with defeat in war, the imperial gatekeepers in 1918 themselves opened the long-barred outer gate to the Social Democrat leaders and admitted them voluntarily, if not without ulterior motives, into the antechambers of power. At this point the Social Democrat masses burst in, overran their leaders, hustled them along and forced open the last doors into the innermost shrine of power. After half a century of waiting, German Social Democracy, in November 1918, seemed to have reached its goal.

Then the incredible happened. Reluctantly raised to the empty throne by the Social Democrat masses, the Social Democrat leaders promptly mobilized the old palace guards and had their own supporters ejected. One year later they themselves were again outside the door – for ever.

The German Revolution of 1918 was a Social Democrat revolution suppressed by the Social Democrat leaders: a process hardly paralleled in the history of the world.

This book intends to describe this process scene by scene. But before we let the curtain rise on the sombre drama, it may be wise to have a brief look at its long prelude: the half-century of Social Democrat hoping and waiting outside the gates of power.

1. *Empire and Social Democracy*

The German Empire and the German Social Democrat Party not only came into being at the same time, they sprouted from the same root: the frustrated middle-class revolution of 1848. This revolution had two aims: national unification and democratic reform. Both were overdue. Germany pre-1848 was based on a proliferation of small states and on feudalism. At the dawn of the industrial age both were ripe for abolition.

But the bourgeois revolution failed, and the German bourgeoisie came to terms with this failure, leaving its tasks to others; Bismarck, at the head of the Prussian Junker class and with the help of the Prussian Army, achieved national unification; the overthrow of outdated regional frontiers. The inner modernization – the overthrow of outdated class barriers – was taken on by the fourth estate, from the enfeebled hands of the third who had left it unfinished. In the 1860s Bismarck and the nascent German workers' movement each held one end of the thread that had snapped off in 1849. If they had worked together, by about 1870 they could have made good what was left undone in 1848: a modern, healthy, lasting German national state might have come into being. But they did not work together, they opposed each other, and this could perhaps hardly have been otherwise – in spite of the brief, fascinating but fruitless flirtation between Bismarck and Lassalle.

The result was a German Empire, powerful and feared by the rest of the world, but at home resembling a wrongly-buttoned waistcoat. Perhaps it was inevitable and pardonable that as a Nation-state it was a little amorphous and imprecise – it excluded many Germans, included many non-Germans. Nor was Bismarck's oddly jumbled and somewhat disingenuous constitution – with its unsolved dualism between Empire and Prussia, its illusory powers of the federal princes and of the Federal Council, its unclear division of omnipotence between Kaiser and Reich Chancellor, its institutionalized impotence of Parliament (the Reichstag), its unintegrated army – the heart of the trouble; constitutions can be changed. To quote Arthur Rosenberg's *History of the German Republic*: 'The Bismarckian empire was mortally ill from the day of its birth' despite the 'glamour of military victories'. What ailed it was a wrong, outdated, anachronistic distribution of power among its classes.

The state was under the wrong management. The Prussian Junkers, who were in a state of economic decline and slowly becoming parasitical, hardly knew what had hit them when they found themselves having to lead a modern industrial state. The capitalist bourgeoisie, which since 1849 had got used to and been spoilt by irresponsibility, was looking abroad for the power withheld from it at home and was pressing for an adventurous foreign policy. And the Social Democrat workers – objectively the nation's strongest reserve strength and willing heirs to the responsibility renounced by the bourgeoisie – counted as 'enemies of the Reich'.

Was this true? They were feared, outlawed, hated, and in the last twelve years of the Bismarck era, from 1878 to 1890, they were persecuted. Beyond doubt they were – in those days – irreconcilably opposed to the administrative and social order Bismarck had given to his Empire. Beyond doubt they proclaimed political and social revolution, about which they admittedly – even then – had no clear notions, let alone concrete plans. Beyond doubt they, like those other 'enemies of the Reich', the Catholic voters of the Centre party, had ties and loyalties beyond the Imperial frontiers: for the latter it was the Catholic Church at large, for them it was the Socialist International.

And yet neither were enemies of the Reich. On the contrary: from the outset the Social Democrats and the Centre were the true Reich parties: they had arisen and grown in the Empire, with the Empire and through the Empire; their roots in it were deeper than those of its Prussian founders. Neither the Social Democrats nor the Centre ever dreamed of dissolving or wishing for the dissolution of the German Empire which was their life element. Rather they felt themselves – the Social Democrats even more than the Centre – from the start to be its heirs apparent. It was only a slight exaggeration for Arthur Rosenberg to write: 'The Social Democratic Party Council became a sort of secret shadow government and August Bebel at the height of his power a shadow-Emperor.'

The Social Democrats of the Bismarckian Empire were revolutionary patriots. They wanted revolution and reconstruction at home – they had no wish for weakness and dissolution in the eyes of the world at large. They wanted to turn Bismarck's Empire into *their* Empire – not to weaken or abolish it, but to raise it to the level of the age. Admittedly, such an attitude, however clear in theory, was in practice not without contradictions. There is a certain contradiction in the two most famous sayings of August Bebel, for years the Party leader: 'For this system not one man nor one penny!' and 'If it's against Russia, I myself will grab a gun!' But this was not the contradiction on which the Social Democrats foundered in 1918; it was quite another.

Until the last moment they promised themselves a German social revolution. In the beginning they genuinely hoped and strove for it; but it remained for them a matter of tomorrow or the day after, never the immediate issue of the day. No German Social Democrat ever asked himself, like Lenin: 'What is to be done?' The Revolution, they kept telling themselves, would sooner or later 'come'; it was not something which one had to make here and now. It was enough to await it; in the meantime they lived in the Kaiser's Empire, things being what they were, as supporters of one of its parties, pleased at the party's growing strength from one Reichstag election to the next. But a revolutionary party which is content to wait for the Revolution gradually ceases to be a revolutionary party. The living day is stronger than the merely hoped-for tomorrow, especially when hopes and expectations recede into an ever more distant future while the present proves increasingly acceptable.

Both these things happened. In 1891 August Bebel had said at the SPD Party Conference: 'Bourgeois society is working so

effectively towards its own downfall that we need merely wait for
the moment to pick up the power dropping from its hands . . .
Yes, I am convinced that the realization of our aims is so close that
there are few in this hall who will not live to see the day.' Twenty
years later he called the Revolution 'the great crashing mess [*der
grosse Kladderadatsch*]' – not exactly the way to describe what you
passionately long for. He was again addressing his bourgeois
opponents, this time in the Reichstag: 'It [the great *Kladderadatsch*] will come not through us, but through you yourselves.'
But there was no longer any talk of the imminence of the day of
revolution. Instead: 'It will come, it is merely adjourned.' This
time there were in fact few in the room who would not live to see
it: seven years later the day was at hand. But at heart the SPD had
ceased genuinely to wish for what it was now calling that great
Kladderadatsch.

It is odd to observe how exactly the critical moments in the
history of the German Empire coincide with those in the history
of the German Social Democrat Party. The forty-eight years of
the *Kaiserreich* embrace three clearly distinct periods: the twenty
years of Bismarck until 1890; the Wilhelminian period from 1890
to 1914; and the four War years from 1914 to 1918. The history
of the Social Democrat Party divides into exactly the same
periods. During the Bismarck period it was or at least considered
itself the party of 'red revolution'. Between 1890 and 1914 it was
revolutionary only in word; at heart it had begun to feel part of
Wilhelminian Germany. In 1914 this change came out into the
open.

Among the reasons for this change the cessation of their persecution was the first. In his last weeks in office Bismarck had
wanted to make the anti-Socialist laws even harsher, to the point
of provoking open civil war. Wilhelm II dropped them instead.
The Social Democrat leaders, who for twelve years had been
outlawed and hunted men, could now lead the safe, pleasant, and
interesting lives of parliamentary notables. They would have had
to be superhuman not to welcome this relaxation with a certain
gratitude.

But that was not all. The whole domestic political atmosphere of Wilhelminian Germany was different from that of the Bismarckian era – more relaxed, less harsh and strict. Germany at the turn of the century was a happier country than she had been in the 1880s. In Bismarck's Germany the air had been heavy to breathe. Wilhelm II had thrown open the windows and let in fresh air; the great and grateful popularity he enjoyed in his early years had not come by accident. Admittedly, this agreeable relaxation at home was achieved by diverting dammed-up energies and excess pressures into foreign fields, at the expense, that is, of the world outside – which was not prepared to put up with this in the long run. In the end War presented the bill.

But around the turn of the century very few would have seen this. What the Social Democrats noticed, more than anybody else, was the disappearance of the sultry atmosphere which had been crying out for a revolutionary thunderstorm. Before 1890 they had really seen the revolution 'coming'. Now they saw it receding into an ever more distant future.

Wilhelminian *Weltpolitik* chiefly favoured the capitalist bourgeoisie who, by contrast with the Bismarck era, were now being compensated for their impotence at home by the deployment of power abroad. But the German worker, too, had a small share in the new wealth of Imperialist expansion. He was still far from well off, but he was better off than before; and a man who notices improvement and hopes for further improvements loses his enthusiasm for revolution. The 'revisionists' in the SPD who in the early years of this century wanted to delete revolution from the Party programme and substitute purely a policy of social reforms had a good nose for the way the wind was blowing. They were outvoted. At its Party conferences and demonstrations the Party went on as ever proclaiming the coming revolution, red flags and all. But the gap between words and feelings was steadily widening. The 'Marxist centre' of the Party secretly agreed with what the revisionists were saying openly; the Party's left wing, which persisted in believing in the revolution, had become a minority.

And then there was a third factor: the SPD's brilliant parliamentary career. With each successive election the Party had gained both voters and mandates. From 1912 onwards it was by far the strongest party in the Reichstag. Could this fail to leave its mark? If the revolution was becoming increasingly improbable while the Social Democrat Parliamentary Party was growing by leaps and bounds in a perfectly legal manner – would this not be food for thought?

Under the Bismarck constitution the Reichstag had little power – but surely this could be changed? Were there not other parties also clamouring for more power? And if power could be achieved by way of a majority in the Reichstag and by constitutional reform in favour of Parliament – what need was there for a revolution? No one, not even the revisionists, said it in so many words, but in fact the SPD of 1914 was already a parliamentary party, no longer a revolutionary one. It no longer wanted to overthrow the existing stage, merely to grow into it, in conjunction with other parliamentary parties, with the Liberals and the Centre. The mass demonstrations and the red flags were now only a traditional ritual. The party's centre of gravity was now in the parliamentary game, in parliamentary ambitions. At the outbreak of war in 1914 it became clear what was appearance and what reality. For one week the SPD kept up revolutionary appearances. On July 25, 1914, in conformity with early Party conference resolutions, it raised 'a fiery protest against the criminal activities of the warmongers'. In the days that followed there were still anti-War demonstrations in the streets of Berlin – demonstrations by no means insignificant: some twenty to thirty thousand people marched each time. Of the two Party Chairmen, one, Friedrich Ebert, travelled to Zurich with the Party funds; they were still anticipating proscription, arrests, confiscations. The other, Hugo Haase, a left-winger, hurried to the offices of the Socialist International in Brussels to consult about international action against the war.

But when War actually broke out, all this was forgotten. With 96 votes against 14 the Parliamentary Party decided to approve the War Credits; and the fourteen dissenters without exception accepted the majority verdict (including, this once, Karl Liebknecht, leftmost of the left-wingers). One of the fourteen was

Hugo Haase, the second Party Chairman, a depressive man who spent his life being outvoted and submitting to the majority will. He was given the job on August 4 of making the famous declaration in the name of the Party and against his inner convictions: 'In its hour of peril we shall not abandon the Fatherland.' The Kaiser gave the equally famous answer: 'I no longer know parties, I know only Germans.' German Social Democracy had made its peace with the *Kaiserreich*. From now on it behaved as if it were a governing party – without being it.

The Party's left wing, faithful to the old revolutionary aims, was shattered by this 'treason' and unable to digest it: in the course of the War it splintered off; sections of the old 'Marxist centre' followed it as did some of the old revisionists, and from 1917 on there were two Social Democrat Parties, the SPD (Social Democrat Party of Germany) and the USPD (Independent Socialist Party of Germany), the 'majority socialists' and the 'Independents', the former loyal to War and State, the latter pacifists and – some of them at least – revolutionaries. But the decision of August 4, 1914 was not 'treason'; it followed logically from the development in the Party's policy during the preceding quarter-century, even if the effects of instinctive patriotism, war-panic and war-fervour are taken into account. The Party rightly understood that the War presented the bill for twenty-five years of aggressive Imperialist foreign policy and that this policy had also profited the German worker and German Social Democracy. It was thus a case of 'in for a penny, in for a pound'. Above all, if with and through Parliament they were to become the party in power, the war would give them their chance. Now for the first time they were *needed*. The party that had the confidence of the masses could not be passed over in a mass war. In saying 'yes' to the war, the SPD believed itself to be crossing the threshold to power.

In this it was both wrong and yet not wrong. Throughout the entire War, to the very last moment, the Reichstag, the Reichstag majority and the Social Democrats failed to get real power – that went to the Military. But in the course of the War the constitutional equilibrium was upset and both the Reichstag and the SPD were among those who gained rather than lost in the transformation. The chief losers were the Kaiser and the Federal princes who from pillars of state became mere ornaments of the constitutional façade. The losers also included the Chancellor and the Cabinet: from responsible decision-makers they turned increasingly into auxiliaries of the High Command.

From autumn 1916 onwards the High Command was Germany's real government. The real Kaiser was now called Hindenburg, the real Chancellor, Ludendorff. But, behind the monarchist façade that was left standing, more evolved than merely a military dictatorship. There was at the same time something approaching a secret republic: the only counterpoise to stay abreast of the Supreme Command, to gain in weight and to compel consideration was the Reichstag majority which in the course of the war shaped itself into a coalition of SPD, Progressive Party, and Centre.

This new constitutional reality revealed itself finally in July 1917 when the High Command and the Reichstag majority did what they had not the least constitutional authority to do: together – if with different long-term aims – they overthrew the Reich Chancellor. Admittedly, against their hopes, it was not the Reichstag majority who decided on his successor. Ludendorff made that decision, and thereby once again showed who was now Germany's real ruler. But at least from 1917 onwards the Reich Chancellor had a Member of Parliament as Vice-Chancellor; the Reichstag majority could no longer be ignored altogether. In the last two war years there was between High Command and Reichstag majority a relationship not unlike that between Government and Opposition in a parliamentary country.

The High Command ruled – and it ruled with an iron fist, with a state of martial law, censorship, and protective custody; far stricter and harsher than the pre-War Imperial constitutional powers it had inconspicuously usurped. But unlike the Imperial authorities before the war, it could no longer simply pass over the parties in the Reichstag majority. They were listened to, they could make themselves heard; they could even overthrow chancellors.

The Reichstag majority was in opposition. There were two issues in constant debate between it and the governing military powers: the War aims and constitutional reform. The Reichstag majority urged a negotiated peace without major annexations. The High Command guaranteed a 'victorious peace'. The Reichstag majority called for free elections to the central Parliament to be held in all the Federal states, for freedom of the press, democratization, parliamentarization. The High Command replied: 'After the victory – perhaps.' At times the debate became acrimonious, and the men of the Reichstag majority had to face vituperation – from their right-wing colleagues in Parliament and from the 'national' press even more than from the Military in power.

This in no way curtailed their loyalty. To the last moment they agreed all War Credits, and the SPD in particular did their best to go on persuading the bleeding and starving masses to 'keep going', in spite of growing discontent and strikes. They never thought of sabotaging the War if it was not waged according to their ideas. That idea occurred only to the Independent Social Democrats, who had organized themselves into a new Party in the spring of 1917 and, although weak in the Reichstag, had considerable influence in the country. They were again what the whole SPD had been under Bismarck: outlaws. Where they were not protected by their parliamentary immunity, they risked protective custody or being drafted as privates into the supply services or into penal battalions.

The men of the Reichstag majority, even the Social Democrats, ran no such risks. They had now become socially acceptable, they frequented the Government offices, even at General Headquarters they were occasionally received and politely listened to. It was an unusual experience for them and the new politeness and accessibility of the mighty could not help but give them a warm and pleasant feeling.

There even developed a sort of camaraderie between certain SPD leaders and some of the men in the new military hierarchy, for instance between Party leader Friedrich Ebert and General Wilhelm Groener. From time to time business threw them together and they got on well with each other; both were the sons of artisans from the South of Germany, the one from Baden, the other from Württemberg; both were serious, sober, able at their jobs and 'nationally-minded men'. Why ever had there been all this hostility in the old days?

The Social Democrat majority party of the war years had grown, if not in fact into power, at least into the atmosphere of power. It was now part of the 'Establishment' even though in the role of an Opposition. It was a national and loyal Opposition and reform party which criticized the Government but had no intention of overthrowing the state. It had come to terms with monarchy and capitalism. A parliamentary form of government and a negotiated peace were its chief remaining aims. It was prepared to alternate peacefully with its right-wing bourgeois opponents in the government of a future parliamentary system; and it was much closer to its bourgeois coalition partners of the Progressive and the Centre Parties than to its ex-comrades of the USPD. The one had become friends and allies; the others had become close enemies.

If one thing suffered from these developments, it was the relationship between Party leadership and Party members. It had always been based on rigid discipline and obedience; the crack about the 'Royal Prussian Social Democrats' was older than the War. But before the war the ordinary 'comrades' and their leaders had still been linked by a good deal of class solidarity, by a sort of pay-day fellowship. The Social Democrat leaders had been ordinary people speaking the language of ordinary people. Now they could occasionally be heard to speak the language of the rulers. While they began to share the concerns of the ruling Military and to value them for their human side, their ordinary supporters were more than ever exposed to the harshness, not to say brutality of a military government. A certain alienation was inevitable. Some of the old SPD strongholds – Berlin, Leipzig, Bremen, Hamburg – now became centres for the new USPD.

The USPD, which since 1916 had been voting against War Credits, continued in the traditions of pre-War Social Democracy much more faithfully than the majority Party. They embraced the entire spectrum of opinions of pre-War Social Democracy, from the revisionist leader Eduard Bernstein via the chief ideologist of the 'Marxist centre' Karl Kautsky, to the internationalist revolutionaries of the 'Spartacist Union', Karl Liebknecht and Rosa Luxemburg. The USPD was by no means a tightly-knit, unified revolutionary party of the Left like Lenin's Russian Bolsheviks. They were united only in their opposition to the War and in their bitter dislike of the war-loyal majority Socialists who heartily reciprocated this dislike. For them the Independents were something like traitors to the Fatherland; for the Independents the majority Socialists were traitors to Socialism and the working class.

But from below, from the ordinary party member's viewpoint, the split which aroused so much bitterness, even hatred among the politicians, seemed pretty harmless. For many of them majority Socialists and Independents were at heart still the same thing, differing only in temper. After all, the majority Socialists were for a negotiated peace, were they not, and against the annexationists and 'War prolongers'; they, too, demanded reforms in the franchise and democracy, only their language was milder and more patient. Also, they too could be approached in cases of personal hardship as a result of martial law, arbitrary arrests and bureaucratic unpleasantness. Perhaps, with their more conciliatory methods, they achieved more than the Independents with their embittered radicalism. Nor had the majority Socialists publicly renounced the great long-range socialist aims.

Confidence dies slowly. The masses still had faith in their old and familiar leaders – those of the SPD hardly less than those of the USPD. These leaders were all they had. During the great strike movement in January 1918 the strikers elected the SPD leaders, too, into the strike leadership – and allowed them after a few days to talk them into ending the strike. After all, there was a War on, and the War would have to be gone through first. Most of the rank and file hoped for a reunification of the Party after the War.

After the War – for the ordinary man in Germany until far into the summer of 1918 – this meant after the victory, or, at worst,

after a negotiated peace. The idea of a possible defeat had never
seriously gained ground. Had there not been an unbroken succession of victories for four years? Was the Army not everywhere in
enemy country? Had not Russia been forced to make peace? For
the people in Germany the War consisted of hunger, worry for
those 'out there' – and news of victories. They kept going,
clenched their teeth and fought and starved and went on toiling –
full of bitterness for those who despite all victories were not ready
to make peace. That they would end by losing the War never
entered their heads.

Indeed there was no one in high places in Germany who had
ever hinted at, let alone admitted, such a possibility. The men at
the top would not admit the possibility of defeat even to themselves, not even in summer 1918 when, after the failure of the last
great German offensive in the West and the massed arrival of the
Americans, it had become almost a certainty. And they wasted the
months when it might have been wise to adjust to imminent
defeat and perhaps still possible to mitigate, if not avoid it.

Then, in August and September, events avalanched. In the West
the Allies went over to the offensive on one sector of the front after
another. The ground gained in the spring was lost, the retreat
gathered pace. Germany's allies collapsed. On September 13
Austria sent out an S.O.S. On September 15 the Allies broke
through on the Balkan front. On September 27 Bulgaria capitulated. On the same day the Allies in the West attacked the
Hindenburg line on a wide front. It was the Germans' last fortified
line of defence and it began to give way.

The German papers were still talking of perseverance and ultimate victory. The parliamentarians in Berlin, full of foreboding
but far from realizing that the end was at hand, discussed whether
the time had not now come to change the Government and to
make an earnest attempt at a negotiated peace. The question was:
how was Ludendorff to be persuaded?

There was a breathtaking surprise in the offing for them. It was
Ludendorff himself who from one day to the next changed the
Government and the Constitution for good measure. He took the
decisions the parliamentarians had not found the strength to take.

He ordered parliamentary democracy in Germany and took the SPD into the government, thus fulfilling its fondest hopes. But by way of a moving-in present he thrust defeat into their hands, and what he was now demanding was not the quest for a negotiated peace – it was capitulation.

The day on which all this happened was September 29, 1918.

2. September 29, 1918

September 29, 1918 was a Sunday. It began as a beautiful late summer day and ended with autumn storms and cloudbursts; in that year it was the day when summer turned into autumn. For Germany it was also the day when the political weather changed. It was the day of the sudden and unheralded decisions which led to the end of the First World War, the end of German resistance and the end of the Kaiser's Empire.

September 29, 1918 is one of the most important dates in German history, but unlike other comparable dates – say January 30, 1933 or May 8, 1945 – it has never ranked as a landmark in German history books. To some extent this may be due to the fact that nothing of what happened on that day was reported in the next day's papers. The events of September 29 remained a state secret for years. Even when they were finally made public, they retained strangely indefinite outlines, as if still shrouded in the fog of secrecy.

September 29, 1918 was May 8, 1945 and January 30, 1933 in one: Capitulation and Reconstruction of the State. Both were the work of *one* man – a man whose constitutional position gave him no authority whatsoever for such far-reaching deeds: Quartermaster-General Erich Ludendorff.[1] September 29, 1918 still preserves the enigma of Ludendorff: the enigma of his power, of his personality and of his motives.

In the last two years of the War Ludendorff's power had become almost unbounded, and its boundlessness never appeared in so harsh a light as on this day when he abjured it and 'broke his staff'. It was a power such as no other German before Hitler had ever possessed, not even Bismarck – dictatorial power.

[1] The British military equivalent to his rank would be 'Deputy Field-Marshal' or Deputy C-in-C.

Ludendorff's nominal superior, the Chief of the High Command, *Generalfeldmarschall* von Hindenburg, was in fact never more than his willing tool. The Kaiser, Supreme Warlord under the terms of the Constitution, had got into the habit of executing, as if it were an order, every wish of the High Command, in the political as well as the military sphere. Chancellors and Ministers came and went as Ludendorff deemed fit. When Ludendorff finally decided from one day to the next to turn Bismarck's Germany into a parliamentary democracy and to have this parliamentary democracy run up the white flag, there was no one to resist or even contradict him; his decision was put into effect with mute efficiency. Yet this man was only one General among many, by no means the highest in rank, only number two in the High Command and without any political office or mandate. What gave him his immense power? Even today there is no clear and uncontested answer to this question, and Ludendorff's character too remains enigmatic: the enigma deepens on closer inspection.

To the man in the street Ludendorff meant nothing at all; he was no popular hero. That was Hindenburg's part and to him Ludendorff freely yielded all the popularity, splendour and glory. Ludendorff was completely free from vanity. One might be tempted to say that he was not interested in the appearance of power, only in power itself – if a closer look did not force the conclusion that power itself also left him unmoved. Has there ever been another dictator who – like Ludendorff on September 29, 1918 – not only voluntarily surrendered power but from the very height of his power commanded and organized its orderly transfer to his political opponents?

Admittedly he did this in the moment of defeat and, as we shall see, not without ulterior motives. Nevertheless, one need only compare Ludendorff's conduct in the moment of defeat with that of Hitler and one will have to admit that whatever Ludendorff was, he was not greedy for power. He was – in a peculiarly harsh, almost evil way – selfless.

Ludendorff was no winner of hearts, no leader of men. He had neither charm nor magnetism; he could no more enchant than he could convince or mesmerize. His manner with people was curt, dry, disagreeable, stand-offish, distant. In his own field, in matters military, he was beyond doubt highly competent, but not the inspired commander that he was later made out to be by his admirers. His talents were less in strategy than in logistics – an organizer and administrator, a technician of war; cool-headed and decisive, ruthlessly conscientious and indefatigable, an able General. But there were other able Generals. If one asks what distinguished this bourgeois General from all others and gave him his incisive power, there is in the end really only one answer: his tough, almost inhuman selflessness which enabled him to become pure will, pure instrument, pure embodiment.

For that is what he was; embodiment, personification – Ludendorff more than anyone else personified the new bourgeois German ruling class which during the War had pushed the old aristocracy increasingly to one side; he embodied its pan-Germanic ideas, its burning desire for victory, the frenzy with which it staked for all or nothing and grasped at world power. Because he was selfless, free from all personal consideration, free in fact from any consideration, because he was completely matter-of-fact in a somewhat sinister, somewhat inhuman way: that is why he was always able to take the utmost risks and make a cool habit of daredevil audacity. That is what Germany's new ruling class could sense, that is why he was their man, why they blindly followed him – while the more sensitively strung aristocrats of the old régime submitted to his merciless objectivity and singleness of purpose and the masses, growling, came to heel.

Ludendorff was the man who undertook not only to win the War for Germany but to win it totally, the man who was prepared to go on playing *va banque* with iron composure. All his decisions were on a colossal scale: the unlimited U-boat war, the support for the Bolshevik Revolution, the forced peace of Brest–Litovsk, the great land-grabbing campaign in the East in the spring and summer of 1918, undertaken at the very moment when he was trying to force a decision in the West: that was his style, a style in which the German *grande bourgeoisie* recognized its own style and an expression of its innermost spirit and aspirations. Ludendorff was the first representative of a new trait in the

German character – a trait of cold frenzy overreaching itself and challenging fate, the 'all or nothing' which became the motto of an entire class and has ever since haunted German history. Ludendorff's unaided decision on September 29 bears the same stamp. It was his characteristic reaction to defeat.

It has often been said, almost from the beginning, that on that day (or rather on the previous Friday, September 27, when the plan took shape in his head which he then put into effect on Sunday) Ludendorff simply 'lost his nerve'. It is true that to the very last moment Ludendorff did not want to acknowledge the defeat which for months had been on the cards, for weeks had been visibly approaching – and then suddenly from one day to the next switched from frantic faith in victory to extreme, perhaps even exaggerated pessimism and defeatism. As late as July he had assured von Hintze, the newly appointed Secretary of State at the German Foreign Office, that the imminent German offensive at Reims would produce final military victory – doubtless trying to keep his own misgivings at bay. At the Imperial Council of August 14, he still held that it would be possible to paralyse the enemy's will to fight by prolonged resistance and agreed to postpone peace feelers until the military situation had improved. Now on September 29 he suddenly demanded a request for an armistice within twenty-four hours – giving as his express reason that he could no longer promise to avoid a military catastrophe on the Western Front for more than twenty-four hours.

Naturally this created the impression that faced with the position at the front, which had indeed become ominous, he had suddenly lost his nerve; especially when in the following days and weeks the feared catastrophe failed to materialize. It is also true that Ludendorff's hardness was a brittle hardness and that earlier in the summer he had had repeated nervous crises which frightened his entourage at headquarters. But characteristically this had happened during those earlier months when against his own better military judgement he had still forced himself to an unjustifiable optimism. On the historic weekend of September 28 and 29 he once again appeared markedly cold, dominating and self-possessed; not like a man who has lost his nerve but rather like one who has recovered it and is pursuing a clearly thought out plan. This was, in fact, the case.

Ludendorff was never a man for caution, for re-insurance, and for keeping all options open. Staff-Officer training and personal temperament, coming together and reinforcing each other, had moulded him to a style of thought and action which knew only clear-cut, extreme alternatives. Ludendorff was in the habit of playing through alternative plans in his mind, Staff-Officer fashion, coming down firmly in favour of one and then implementing the chosen plan with the utmost energy, to the very limit, without so much as glancing to the right or left; if the plan failed, then was the time for new alternatives and new radical decisions. What had tortured Ludendorff in the summer of 1918 and sometimes brought him to the brink of nervous collapse, had probably been the very fact that at that time he found himself condemned to unplanned muddling through. Unable to face the possibility of defeat he had frantically kept on pursuing a victory to which he no longer saw a clear road. Now, suddenly, on September 27 when the Allies breached the Hindenburg line, there was an end to evasion. His military judgement forced him to accept the possibility of immediate military catastrophe. He turned and faced defeat. The shock of the realization must have been terrible but it was also liberating: for now Ludendorff could plan again. Now he planned the defeat.

He planned it as earlier he had planned victory: as a military man, as a General, not as a politician. In the face of defeat he concentrated on one aim: to save the Army.

Every war gives rise to a subtle conflict between the political and the military leadership. Victory sometimes glosses over this; defeat mercilessly lays it bare. Sometimes when a law-suit is being lost there comes a moment when a lawyer thinks less about the interests of his client than about how he can protect himself against his disappointed client's claims for redress. In much the same way in the moment of defeat the leaders of a beaten army often think no longer of the interests of the country they can no longer protect but only of how to preserve their military honour. Thus it was in France in 1940, and thus it was in Germany in 1918.

From the moment when he began to plan 'Operation Defeat' Ludendorff had one fixed goal: to save the Army – its existence and its honour. To save the *existence* of the Army, an armistice had to be concluded – as soon as possible, without delay, by tomorrow if possible; every day might bring military collapse. But to save the *honour* of the Army the request for an armistice would have to come from the Government, not from the High Command. It would have to be based on political, not on military grounds. This aim generated three questions: where were those political grounds to be found? What Government would be prepared to shoulder the burden? And how could one make sure that the victorious enemy would indeed grant the requested armistice?

The answers to these questions converged. To appear politically motivated, the request for an armistice would have to be linked with an offer of peace and would therefore have to come from those who had long advocated a negotiated peace; i.e., the majority parties in the Reichstag. These parties would therefore have to join the Government or form one. To get the Reichstag majority to assume the burden of government under such dreadful conditions, they would have to be tempted: that meant the change in the Constitution on which they placed so much value, the transition towards a parliamentary form of government. This would at the same time improve the chances for an armistice. The *Entente* were claiming to fight for democracy; President Wilson, in particular, had several times publicly proclaimed the democratization of Germany as the chief aim of the war. Excellent! If he was now handed a German democratic Government on a plate he could hardly refuse its petition for an armistice. To make it even harder for him to refuse, his famous 14 Points would be accepted as a basis for peace negotiations.

And if, nevertheless, he refused – or came up with new, unforeseen, dishonourable conditions? Well, one would have to see. Perhaps the new popular Government would then unleash a people's war, a desperate *levée en masse*. But if they did not do that and submitted instead – then it would be *their* submission; the Army in any case was safe; its existence as well as its honour. With its existence intact and its honour unstained, it could later, after the War, send packing a parliamentary Government disgraced by capitulation.

That was the plan – Ludendorff's plan for the manipulation of the defeat which he now saw as inevitable. He formed it on September 27. On September 28 he took Hindenburg into his confidence who, as usual, agreed. On September 29 he gained one by one the assent of the Foreign Minister, the Kaiser and the Chancellor. It was Ludendorff's last great operation; in contrast with his great military offensives of 1918, he achieved a complete breakthrough at the first attempt this time.

*

The operation was executed with military precision, with the element of surprise playing a decisive role. Until Friday evening nobody had even an inkling of what was in Ludendorff's mind. On the morning of September 28 he began by informing the Reich Chancellor, the aged Count Hertling, through his Berlin liaison officer Colonel von Winterfeldt, that the High Command had formed the opinion 'that a reconstruction of the Government or its extension on a broader base had become necessary'. At the same time he ordered the Reich Chancellor to come immediately to General Headquarters. Count Hertling's son and A.D.C. reports: 'Immediately after Colonel von Winterfeldt had left his room, my father came to me and reported the sudden change in the High Command's political views. I was, of course, very surprised to learn from him that from one day to the next the High Command had espoused the cause of parliamentarianism to which they had never before subscribed.' The Chancellor decided to travel that evening. The Secretary of State at the Foreign Office, Paul von Hintze, went ahead of him. It was Saturday morning, September 28. Only late in the afternoon, when this step had already been taken, did Ludendorff consider it necessary to acquaint Hindenburg, his nominal superior, of his intentions.

In his memoirs he has this to say:

On 28 September, at 6 p.m., I went down to the next landing to call on the *Generalfeldmarschall* in his room. I gave him an exposé of my thoughts about an offer of peace and armistice ... We now had the one

Above: Kaiser Wilhelm II (c) with (l) von Hindenburg and (r) Ludendorff at military head-quarters during the First World War. (*Photo: Ullstein*)

Right: General Erich Ludendorff, second in rank in the Military High Command. (*Photo: Heinrich Hoffman*)

Above: Friedrich Ebert, as Reich President, followed by Reich Chancellor Wirth and General Seekt (in military cap), taking a parade. (*Photo: Staatsbibliotek, Berlin*)

Below: Gustav Noske, Commander-in-Chief of the *Freikorps*, military units formed for the purpose of suppressing the Revolution, addresses a meeting during the Berlin elections. (*Photo: Staatsbibliotek, Berlin*)

task to act with dispatch, clarity and determination. The *Generalfeld-marschall* listened to me deeply moved. He replied that he had wanted to say the same thing to me that evening, he too had constantly reviewed the position in his mind and considered this step necessary . . . The *Generalfeldmarschall* and I parted with a firm handshake like men who have buried the thing they love and who intend to stick together not only in life's good moments but also in its heaviest hours.

This description does not make it clear whether Ludendorff revealed his entire plan to his Chief or whether – as is more probable – he disclosed to him only the military side of it as he had earlier disclosed only the political side to the Chancellor.

It is, however, known that on Sunday morning Ludendorff discussed the entire plan in all its details with von Hintze who arrived during the night. On this we have Hintze's testimony; it is even possible that Ludendorff's plan was further modified during this conversation and that Hintze's contribution gave it its final shape. Hintze much resembled Ludendorff in his mental make-up; a youngish man, he was incisive, unflappable, and sharp-witted, a naval officer by training and, like Ludendorff, of bourgeois origin and pan-Germanic views. When Ludendorff told him bluntly that the Western Front might collapse at any minute and that the situation of the Army demanded an immediate armistice, he was 'crushed' but quickly took hold of himself. Not only did he approve of Ludendorff's suggestion that the request for an armistice should be the responsibility of the majority in the Reichstag, he went even further. Ludendorff had evidently thought at first only of inviting representatives of the Social Democrats, the Progressive Party and the Centre Party to join the existing Government in order to justify the sudden request for an armistice and offer of peace. Hintze felt this was not enough. In view of the 'catastrophic effect on army, people, empire and monarchy' which might ensue, it would be better to have a complete, visible, dramatic change in the system, an immediate change in the constitution, a 'revolution from above'. (This expression was first used in this conversation although it is not clear whether by Hintze or by Ludendorff.) Ludendorff was at first afraid this would delay the armistice, but then he quickly absorbed the Secretary of

2

State's thinking. A 'revolution from above' – that made sense; it appealed to his inclination for the radical all-or-nothing approach; it dotted the *i*'s of his plan. The more complete the break with the present Government and Constitution, the more credible it would be that the request for an armistice arose from the personal political aspirations of the New Men – and that the Army had nothing to do with it. Hindenburg was consulted and, as ever, agreed. Lunch followed. The afternoon had been set aside for the report to the Kaiser.

*

Meanwhile the unsuspecting Reich Chancellor, the old Count Hertling, was on his way to Spa, the Belgian resort where the General Headquarters had been located for some time. He was accompanied by his son who has left a graphic account of the journey and what happened on arrival:

It was a beautiful, warm and sunny day. It felt strange, passing through that familiar region which we had come to love and had left just a month ago. Autumn had moved into the countryside, the woods glowed in all colours . . . As we approached Spa, the weather changed, dark clouds loomed up and as we drove into our castle, a fine drizzle began to fall from the sky. The house was cold and unwelcoming.

We had not long arrived when Herr von Hintze had himself announced. His conversation with my father was brief. When he left, my father, looking very serious, came into my room and said: 'It's quite terrible, the High Command demand that *as soon as ever possible* a peace offer be made to the *Entente*. Hintze's pessimism has been proved right!'

The old Chancellor had decided en route to offer his resignation. He had been a convinced monarchist all his life. He did not want to have a hand in ushering in a parliamentary régime. It never occurred to him that he could thwart Ludendorff's request. And now this as well! As a patriot he was shaken. As a Chancellor determined to resign anyhow, he was perhaps relieved that it was, as it were, no longer his business.

At Hindenburg's decisive interview with the Kaiser the Reich Chancellor was not even present. Civilian Government was represented only by Hintze who since that morning had been in full

agreement with Hindenburg and Ludendorff. The Kaiser himself
made no attempt at resistance, he approved everything; both the
change in the Constitution as well as the plea for an armistice.
The only thing he provisionally rejected was Hintze's offer of
resignation.

Thus, when the Kaiser with his entourage finally called on the
aged Reich Chancellor at 4 p.m., everything had already been
decided. All that was left to do was to draft the Imperial Decree on
constitutional change and to accept Count Hertling's resignation.
The most striking thing about the events of this historic day is the
undramatic and subdued smoothness with which everything happened as if taken for granted. It was after all a question of
admitting defeat after four years of passionately contested world
war and of tearing down at the same time Bismarck's constitutional edifice. But no one seemed to get excited and only the
resignations of the Chancellor and the Secretary of State caused
some debate. Ludendorff had taken them all by surprise, and they
all played their allotted role as if in a trance, not noticing the
immensity of their actions.

The younger Hertling recorded:

The Kaiser seemed to me on this day to look no worse than usual . . .
the meeting took a long time. Herr von Hintze who had spent the night
travelling to Spa and the whole morning negotiating with the High
Command, looked completely exhausted and as a result of this over-
exertion fell asleep in our room while waiting to be called to consultation . . . Meanwhile the Kaiser's declaration had been drafted, in which
he expressed his intention of giving representatives of the people a
greater part in the business of Government and in which he graciously
accepted my father's resignation. I brought the document into the study
where the momentous discussion was still going on. The Kaiser did not
say much; the Chief of his Cabinet Office spoke for him, with such
animation that his voice was clearly audible in the next room. The
Kaiser was more than pained by the Chancellor's resignation . . . Then
the discussion ended. As ever the Kaiser took amiable leave of us all
and we were alone. My father was pretty quiet. But when I reminded
him how we would now soon move from the 'lowlands' of Prussia
into the high plateau of our beloved Bavarian mountains, a gentle
almost happy smile flittered across his grave face.

And the Kaiser? According to his chronicler Niemann, 'on the evening of September 29 there was a feeling of quiet resignation among the Imperial entourage, accompanied however by unmistakable disgruntlement with General Ludendorff.' Quiet resignation and 'unmistakable' disgruntlement was all that Kaiser and Chancellor could muster on that fateful day to oppose the will of Ludendorff – they did not dare to protest.

The constitutional authorities of the *Kaiserreich* capitulated on September 29, 1918 without a battle; in a certain sense they had already abdicated. There was more battle done in the days to follow in Berlin during the formation of the parliamentary Government which, in assuming power, was to take on the responsibility for the defeat; and in the High Command the decisions of September 29 hit the staff officers like a bomb, when they learnt about them the next day.

3. October

'Dreadful and terrible!' Colonel von Thaer noted in his diary on October 1, the day after the meeting at which Ludendorff had told the entire staff of the High Command what had happened. The diary adds: 'While Ludendorff was speaking one could hear muted groaning and sobbing, many, perhaps most, had tears helplessly running down their cheeks . . . As I had a previous appointment to report to him afterwards, I followed him at once and – being an old acquaintance – grasped him by the right upper arm with both hands, a thing I might have hesitated to do under different circumstances, and said: "Excellency, can this really be true? Is this the last word? Am I awake or dreaming? It's simply too terrible! What is to become of us?" '

Scenes very similar to this occurred the next morning in the Reichstag in Berlin when an emissary of Ludendorff's, Major von dem Bussche, told all the party leaders: 'The High Command has found it necessary to urge his Majesty to try to break off the fighting, to give up the continuation of the war as hopeless. Every day might worsen the position and reveal our basic weakness to the enemy.'

An eye-witness account describes the effect:

The deleg ates were shattered; Ebert turned deathly pale and could not utter a word; the delegate Stresemann looked as if he were about to have a fit . . . Minister von Waldow is said to have left the room with the words: 'All that is left now is to put a bullet through one's head.' Herr von Heydebrand, the leader of the Prussian Conservatives, rushed into the corridor shouting: 'For four years we have been lied to and deceived!'

While he thus drew into confusion both the general staff and the Reichstag – the two centres of power between which the game of

German politics was from now on to be played – Ludendorff himself had completely regained his composure. He once again felt master of the situation and planned with his customary cool precision. Colonel von Thaer – whose diary is invaluable as the only more or less literal account of Ludendorff's utterances in those days – gives this description of his appearance:

When we had assembled, Ludendorff stepped among us, his face filled with the deepest grief, pale, but with his head held high. A truly beautiful Germanic hero figure! I had to think of Siegfried with the fatal wound in his back from Hagen's spear.

He said roughly this: It was his duty to tell us that our military situation was terribly grave. Our Western Front might be breached any day ... There was *no* relying on the troops any longer ... Thus it was to be anticipated that in the near future with the help of the high battle morale of the Americans the enemy would gain a *major* victory, a *break-through on a very large scale*; our army in the West would then get out of control and flood back across the Rhine in complete disorder, bringing revolution to Germany. This catastrophe *had* to be prevented at all costs. For the above reasons no further defeat could be risked. The High Command had therefore requested H.M. and the Chancellor to apply *without any delay* to Wilson, the American President, for an armistice with a view to concluding peace on the basis of his 14 Points ...

It had been a terrible moment for the Field Marshal and for him to have to make this announcement to H.M. and to the Chancellor. The latter, Count Hertling, had informed H.M. in a dignified manner that he would have to offer his immediate resignation. After so many honourable years he could not and would not now, as an old man, end his life pleading for an armistice. The Kaiser had accepted his resignation.

His Excellency Ludendorff added: 'For the moment we are therefore without a Chancellor. It is not yet clear who will take over. *I have however begged H.M. now to draw into the Government those circles whom we have chiefly to thank for being in this position.* We shall thus see these gentlemen moving into the Ministries. Let them conclude the peace that *must* now be concluded. Let them cope with the mess! It is *their* mess after all.'

And when von Thaer afterwards grabbed him by the arm, 'he remained completely calm and gentle and said with a profoundly sad smile: "This, alas, is how things are and I can see no other way out." '

*

The 'way out' which Ludendorff saw and which allowed him to remain 'completely calm and gentle' was none other than the shifting of the responsibility for defeat which was later to give rise to the legend of the stab-in-the-back. For who had got whom into a mess here? If the German defeat on September 29 was really as total as Ludendorff claimed, then it was *his* defeat, for it was he who until that day had determined Germany's conduct and policy of war; he, not his critics. But if the defeat was not yet total and the request for an armistice premature, then more than ever it was *his* defeat: for then he brought it about by suing for the armistice. If the other side still had doubts about winning, if Germany still questioned her defeat, and if therefore the winning side was still ready to negotiate, the losing side still ready to resist, the request for an immediate armistice was bound to nullify all this. It meant waving the white flag. It was Ludendorff who insisted that this should now happen but it was not he who would shoulder the blame; the new Government of the Reichstag majority should 'cope with the mess'. It was his price for letting them govern.

Ludendorff in the moment of his defeat was the same coldly daring planner that he had always been. As always he bid for a grand slam. He offered the majority parties in the Reichstag what they had not hoped for even in their wildest dreams: complete parliamentary government, full power. An irresistible bait! True, the bait was poisoned: it comprised the responsibility for defeat, the total defeat which had become inevitable through the request for an armistice. Ludendorff baited a trap for his political opponents, as he had done for the Russians at Tannenberg, and like the Russians at Tannenberg, they blundered into it – even if at first they sniffed at it suspiciously and shrank back. Prince Max von Baden, the new Reich Chancellor, a liberal Prince who in preceding years had cautiously criticized Ludendorff's conduct of the War, was thunderstruck when he learnt on his arrival in Berlin on October 1 what was expected from him. For a few days he fought a desperate battle against the request for an armistice; thus it went off only on October 4, not on the 1st as Ludendorff had demanded. Philipp Scheidemann, then number two in the Social Democrat party and their expert in the Reichstag on Foreign Affairs, argued prophetically at a meeting of the Parliamentary Party against stepping into 'a bankrupt enterprise', and a large part of those present supported him.

The two men who broke the resistance of Prince Max and of the Social Democrats were, strange to say, the present and the future head of state. At a Privy Council meeting Wilhelm II barked at his reluctant fellow prince: 'You have not come here to make difficulties for the High Command.' And Friedrich Ebert, the leader of the Social Democrat Party, argued at the Party meeting that the Party should not lay itself open to the accusation of having refused its co-operation at a time when it was being urgently begged for it from all sides. 'On the contrary we must throw ourselves into the breach. We must see whether we can get enough influence to push through our demands, and if it is possible to do this and at the same time save the country, then it is our damned duty to do it.' Ebert won – and sent the reluctant Scheidemann as Secretary of State into the Government of Prince Max.

So Germany learnt on the morning of October 5 that from now on it was a parliamentary democracy, that it had a new Government in which, under a liberal Prince as Chancellor, the Social Democrats, the '*Scheidemen*', called the tune; and that as its very first act this Government had addressed an immediate petition for peace and an armistice to the American President. Nobody was told anything of what had happened on September 29. That Ludendorff was behind the request for an armistice, that he had practically forced it through, of this no one in Germany outside a tiny closed circle had the least suspicion. In any event such a suspicion would have seemed absurd. Hindenburg and Ludendorff – were they not the men with the strong nerves and the iron resolve to achieve victory, the self-appointed guarantors of the ultimate triumph? Scheidemann on the other hand, and the Centre Party delegate Matthias Erzberger, both now suddenly in the Government, were undoubtedly the men behind the Reichstag 'peace resolution' of July 1917, the 'lily-livered, muck-raking pictures of misery, birds of ill omen, Jeremiahs croaking from the depths', as a Conservative proclamation called them by way of greeting. It was just like them, now that things were in a bad way, immediately to cry for peace! For years the battle about the War aims had been waged in Germany under the two slogans of 'Hindenburg's peace' and 'Scheidemann's peace'. Now Scheidemann was in the Government – and here at once was the capitulation. There you have it. This way it was bound to happen. With a Government like this the war was over – and lost.

The other news, the announcement of a far-reaching change in the constitution, was almost eclipsed by these terrible tidings. Admittedly Ebert, in the Reichstag, celebrated October 5 as a 'turning point in Germany's history' and the 'birthday of German democracy', but hardly anyone listened. At this moment constitutional changes left the German masses comparatively indifferent, and a Prince as Reich Chancellor did not look much like democracy. What counted was the end of the War, the defeat, capitulation, the end of the terror and the terror of the end. With lightning speed the whole country was divided into two camps. The one heard the news with relief, the other with despair. The masses, hungry and tired of war, breathed with relief; the bellicose middle class, thirsting for victory, stifled a sob. The one groaned: 'At last!' The other groaned: 'Treason!' And at once the two camps began to view each other with hatred. All were agreed on one thing only: this was the end.

On just this point, however, they were all wrong. The end was slow in coming. The whole of October passed. The petition for an armistice had been addressed to President Wilson who had to consult his Allies and who in any case reacted with hesitation and mistrust, dosing out his conditions drop by drop. Between October 8 and 23 he sent three notes. The first demanded, as a precondition, retreat from the occupied territories. The second demanded cessation of the U-boat war. The third was a scarcely veiled demand for the Kaiser's abdication. Meanwhile the War continued. Men went on dying on the Western Front, went on starving at home. During this month of October 1918, orders to

2*

report to the Army still went out in large numbers: the seventeen-year-olds were being drafted.

Every reply to Wilson was the subject of prolonged wrangling in Berlin, and between Berlin and Headquarters in Spa. Positions became strangely reversed.

*

In the first week of October the Reich Chancellor had desperately resisted the request for an armistice and Ludendorff had peremptorily insisted on it. But now that it had been dispatched, the Government felt committed to it whereas Ludendorff increasingly withdrew from his original position. Now he suddenly favoured breaking off the exchange of notes and carrying on the fight – and this in spite of the fact that Germany's situation was becoming daily more desperate.

True, the great Allied breakthrough of the Western Front which Ludendorff had feared at the end of September had failed to materialize. The Western Front wavered and fell back but it did not break, neither through the whole of October nor in November; on the very day of the armistice there was still a coherent German Front in the West, albeit in full retreat and without hope of halting. But Germany's last allies, Austria-Hungary and Turkey, collapsed in the course of October, and from the Balkans and Italy unopposed Allied armies approached Germany's unprotected southern borders. The loss of Rumanian oil made the day inevitable when Army transport, fighter planes and the Navy would come grinding to a halt. Even if in the West it might have been remotely possible to drag things out into the winter – a spring campaign was out of the question.

It would be underestimating Ludendorff's military judgement to suggest that he alone failed to grasp this. By the second half of October he, like everyone else, must have known that defeat could really no longer be postponed and that an early armistice offered the only chance of sparing the country at least the horrors of invasion. And yet Ludendorff chose this moment to advocate a last-ditch stand – as if September 29 had never been.

For Ludendorff's *volte-face* there is no military explanation nor one based on external politics, only one based on domestic politics. Ludendorff was no friend of parliamentary democracy. It is true that he had himself decreed a parliamentary government on September 29 – but surely not in order to turn it into a successful and permanent institution, merely to mark it with the stamp of defeat and capitulation and, once it had done its job, to be sure of quickly overthrowing it. His first step had succeeded beyond expectations. The new Parliamentary Government had assumed full responsibility for the request for an armistice and shielded the High Command from any suspicion of paternity. As late as October 16 the Government issued this directive at its press conference: 'The impression that our peace move originates from the military must be avoided at all costs. The Reich Chancellor and the Government have undertaken to sponsor this step. The press must not destroy this impression.' This loyal self-denial was the Government's attempt at a patriotic bluff *vis-à-vis* the enemy; if possible no one in America, England and France was to notice until the last moment that the High Command itself had given the War up for lost. But with this very step the Parliamentary Government left itself at the High Command's mercy; if it insisted on having waved the white flag of its own accord, it left the High Command free to protest against such feeble and shameful defeatism, thus preparing the way for the subsequent reproach of the stab-in-the-back – and this with increasing impunity as the situation became more and more obviously irretrievable.

From the middle of October onwards Ludendorff found himself again able to play the heroic part of the unconquered and belligerent soldier manfully resisting a peace-seeking Government of weak-kneed democrats ready to surrender.

*

He had come to terms with Wilson's first note. After the second note he rumbled discontent and refused to take any responsibility for an assenting reply. After the third one, he issued, on October 24, without so much as waiting for the Government's reaction, an order-of-the-day on his own authority, in which he said the note was unacceptable and could 'only be a challenge for us soldiers to continue resistance with our utmost strength'. But in so doing Ludendorff had overbid his hand. The unexpected happened – Prince Max von Baden the Reich Chancellor, an aristocratic, rather gentle person and by nature no real fighter – stood his ground. He presented the Kaiser with an ultimatum: 'Ludendorff has to go – or I go.' And this time it was Ludendorff who had to go.

On October 17, during a Cabinet meeting at which Ludendorff was present, Prince Max 'lost confidence in Ludendorff as a man': 'Today General Ludendorff did not breathe a word about the armistice offer and its disastrous effect on Germany and on the outside world, while he treated the armistice conversations in Berlin as responsible for the encouragement of the enemy and the deterioration of the morale at the Front.' Perhaps the Prince did not quite see through the whole of the insidious game Ludendorff intended to play with the Government; but with the instinct of the aristocrat from a ruling house he sensed something disloyal, autocratic, unreliable in Ludendorff's *volte face*. The order of the day of October 24 and a second journey to Berlin, undertaken by Hindenburg and Ludendorff on the following day against the Chancellor's express wish, were the last straw: 'It was clear to me that this journey could only end in General Ludendorff's dismissal. This piece of defiance only gave me the occasion I needed. I was also influenced by a desire to ease the internal and external situation. *But it was my loss of confidence in him that was really decisive.*'

Suddenly it emerged that in such a crisis between Government and High Command Ludendorff was no longer the stronger. By pushing through the request for an armistice he had himself sawn off the branch on which he was sitting. For two years his unbounded power had been based on his being the man who guaranteed victory. When he stopped doing this, he was merely a General like all the others. Before September 29 Ludendorff could get what he wanted at every point in the conflict by merely threatening to resign. When he now did it again, he lived to hear the Kaiser say: 'Well, if you insist on going, by all means go.' This happened on October 26 at 10 a.m., at an audience in the

Bellevue Palace in Berlin where the Kaiser received Ludendorff and Hindenburg 'very ungraciously'. The Kaiser suddenly levelled reproaches at Ludendorff – because of the offer of an armistice, and also because of the unauthorized order of the day of October 24 – and told him bluntly he had lost confidence in him.

Ludendorff had a last ace up his sleeve – or thought he had. When the Kaiser so casually accepted the General's resignation,

The Field Marshal [Hindenburg] dropped his habitual reticence and likewise offered his resignation which the Kaiser rejected by remarking brusquely: 'You stay on!' The Field Marshal bowed before this imperial decision. The Kaiser had hardly left the room when a brief but heated exchange ensued between Hindenburg and Ludendorff who reproached the Field Marshal for leaving him in the lurch in this decisive hour. When, on getting into his car, the Field Marshal invited him to join him for the return journey, he refused and returned to Staff Headquarters alone.

Ludendorff told this, immediately after the audience, to Colonel von Haeften who has left this record.

In this dismal fashion ended the dictatorship of General Ludendorff.

*

A month earlier this event would have shaken the German public like no other. Now it aroused little attention. Events had already left the person of Ludendorff behind. For not only the War situation but also Germany's internal mood and state of affairs had changed immensely in the weeks since the request for an armistice. 'Two attitudes of mind', the Saxon envoy in Berlin reported to his ministry, 'dominate the masses. One is an extreme longing for peace; the other an unmistakable bitterness about the fact that previous Governments failed to appreciate the limits of German power and so fed the belief in German invincibility, that large sections of the population had a false sense of security.' Longing for peace, then, and a crisis of confidence, together with the certainty since October 5 that the War was lost and all further sacrifices were in vain: these resulted in an incalculable, explosive mood among the masses. Add to this that the days passed and the overdue armistice stayed out of reach, and the result was impatience – a bitterly tense, almost unbearable impatience.

The talk everywhere was about the notes in which President Wilson cast doubts upon Germany's sudden democratic metamorphosis and urged further internal changes. The exchange of notes between Prince Max's Government and the American President was probably the strangest that has ever preceded an armistice between warring powers. It reminds one of an academic controversy between constitutional lawyers of different persuasions. The German notes kept asserting that since the October constitutional reform the German Government no longer represented an autocratic régime but was responsible solely to the people and their freely elected Parliament. The President was not quite ready to believe this – and no wonder. 'Significant and important as the constitutional changes seem to be which are spoken of by the German Foreign Secretary in his note of the 20th October', Wilson said in his reply three days later, 'it does not appear that the principle of a Government responsible to the German people has yet been fully worked out, or that any guarantees either exist or are in contemplation that the alterations of principle and of practice now partially agreed upon will be permanent . . . It is evident that the German people have no means of commanding the acquiescence of the military authorities of the Empire in the popular will; that the power of the King of Prussia to control the policy of the Empire is unimpaired; that the determining initiative still remains with those who have hitherto been the masters of Germany.' He certainly was not all that far off the mark. Originally a professor of political science, Wilson may have been doctrinaire, his (perfectly sincere) view of the War as a crusade for democracy may have smacked of the quixotic: his analysis of the situation inside Germany nevertheless went straight to the heart of the matter. Did not the brand-new Parliamentary democracy exist in fact merely by the grace of the High Command? Was it really firmly in the saddle as long as the country everywhere was still living under a state of emergency and the

Generalkommandos[1] held sway? Was Prince Max's Government anything more than a thin parliamentary veil over the old reality, owing its existence as it did to a 'revolution from above'?

Since Wilson's third note everyone in Germany was suddenly bandying two phrases about which a bare three weeks ago no one had yet heard: 'Kaiser-problem' and 'Revolution'. If the Kaiser's presence was an obstacle to an armistice – should he not make the sacrifice and abdicate? This question was suddenly being asked not only by Social Democrat workers, but also by confirmed monarchists; not only by the people, but also by Ministers. It was not yet a debate about 'Monarchy or Republic'; on the contrary many men in responsible positions, including the Reich Chancellor, saw the Kaiser's abdication as the best, perhaps the only way to save the monarchy. They calculated that a Regency and an early armistice might still preserve the state, the constitution and the monarchy. But if the 'Kaiser-problem' wrecked the armistice, the threat of revolution loomed.

No one as yet knew how and from what direction revolution would come. But it was in the air, sinister and intangible, and the presence of the 'Kaiser-problem' threatened to spark it off. It was feared that the masses would rise in despair to get rid of the Kaiser who was standing between them and peace – and if they did, they would sweep away everything else along with him: monarchy, state, army and navy, Government and authority, aristocracy and *grande bourgeoisie*.

This had to be prevented. Prince Max von Baden was not alone in thinking so, Friedrich Ebert thought the same. He, too, was deeply worried by the threatening revolution. Defeat from the outside was now inevitable and was bad enough. *Defeat from the outside and Revolution on the inside* – that was too much, more than one could cope with. The very thought filled Ebert with horror. He now shared the aims of the Government which he supported with all his strength: the Kaiser's abdication – an early armistice – a Regency – the preservation of the monarchy.

[1] Translator's note: Since the beginning of the war, the General commanding a Home Command had exercised supreme authority over the civilians within his command, dividing the country into *Generalkommandos*.

The Kaiser himself had no intention of abdicating but he, too, was afraid of revolution: for that very reason he now desired the armistice as eagerly as the people and the Government. He needed the Army to smash the revolution at home if it should break out. That presupposed the armistice. The Army must no longer be tied down to fighting the enemy; it would have to be free to turn and march against the rebellious homeland. If Ludendorff still wanted to stop this he had to go. The Kaiser already had his eye on the Commander who would quell the revolution: General Wilhelm Groener, a clear-headed man from Swabia who might be expected to take in his stride the military defeat which was not of his making, but who would restore law and order at home with a firm hand. On October 30 the Kaiser unceremoniously left Berlin, escaping the tactless discussions of his abdication in the capital, and took up battle stations at General Headquarters, surrounded by his military paladins.

*

A no-man's-land in time, this month of October 1918 – a time between War and Peace, between Empire and Revolution, between military dictatorship and Parliamentary democracy. As the month advanced, the normal political bearings became increasingly shrouded as if in a fog. The individual protagonists lost sight of each other – were almost out of earshot from each other; each obsessed with his own fear – the Kaiser fearing for his throne, the High Command for the coherence of the Army, the Chancellor for a timely armistice, the Social Democrat leaders for the patience of the masses. A few conspirators did put their heads together in Berlin (and only there) and planned revolutionary action, originally for November 4, then for November 11. They too were full of fear – for the feasibility of their plans. For although everyone was talking of the possibility of a revolution, nobody knew whether the masses were really ready and able to revolt; and nobody knew what powers of resistance the Establishment might yet muster if an uprising took place.

In the event it was not the Berlin conspirators who set the Revolution in motion, and it was not the 'Kaiser-problem' which sparked it off, but a totally unexpected act of despair by the Naval Command.

For an understanding of this step, let us listen once more to the voice of Ludendorff. Ludendorff had departed – to Sweden on a forged passport – but his spirit survived in the Army and Navy staffs. On October 31 Ludendorff wrote down what was now in his mind:

Certainly our situation was no longer capable of improvement. In the South-East disaster was, beyond doubt, taking its course. But a last effort by the German people would have had a sobering effect on the people and armies of France, England and probably also America. For a few months we could have kept the War going. A fortress which surrenders before making a last-ditch stand is cursed with dishonour. A people which accepts humiliations and submits to conditions destructive of its existence, without having pitted its last strength, is courting its final downfall. If it submits to a similar fate after making a last supreme effort, it will live.

Much of this is unrealistic and illogical, but it contains *one* genuine feeling. Of course one cannot survive the destruction of one's existence, even after a last-ditch stand, and anyway Wilson's conditions included no such thing. That Germany might have 'kept the War going for a few months' could perhaps have applied before September 29; not now. But when Ludendorff talks of 'the curse of dishonour' which strikes those who stop fighting before they are totally unable to fight, he touches upon something that was real and alive. A specific concept of honour which was then deeply ingrained in the German Officers' Corps, indeed in the German ruling class; a concept of honour which, though it is rigid and formal and nowadays seems somewhat archaic and moth-eaten, was in those days a powerful psychological reality. It governed the thoughts, emotions and actions of the German ruling class for whom it established their identity and distinguished them from the masses, who were not gentlemen, had no honour and could not be challenged to a duel. This concept of honour divided upper and lower classes into two separate worlds. Strange that Ludendorff had forgotten it completely on September 29; less surprising that he was now remembering it.

Others had never forgotten it, even then. Let us recall how his own staff officers reacted to his decision to capitulate: 'One could hear muted groaning and sobbing, many, perhaps most, had tears helplessly running down their cheeks.' They felt dishonoured. The masses at home, as also the masses of simple soldiers and sailors might feel relieved by the prospect of peace and life, even if the War was lost, even if the fight was abandoned before the last ditch; not so the officers. For them surrender meant disgrace; and to disgrace they preferred death. And the other ranks would have to join in the dying without reasoning why.

But the other ranks no longer wanted to go on dying – not now that the War had been given up as lost, and not for the sake of the honour of one class, an honour in which they did not share and which meant nothing to them – and this, not the 'Kaiser-problem', in fact, now triggered off the Revolution.

When the naval officers tried in earnest to mount a last-ditch stand, the sailors mutinied – and swept the home Army and the workers along with them. What was rising up here was an elemental desire to live, and what it was rising against was an extravagant conception of honour clamouring for an end wreathed in glory. Three days after Ludendorff's dismissal, two days after the acceptance of Wilson's last note, while the Government was busy getting rid of the Kaiser and saving the monarchy, and while the German armistice delegation was packing its bags, in Germany the earth began to shake.

4. The Revolution

The first historian of the Weimar Republic, Arthur Rosenberg, has called the November Revolution of 1918 'the weirdest of all revolutions . . . The masses backing the majority parties in the Reichstag rebelled against the Max von Baden Government, that is to say, in fact against themselves.' Rosenberg's analysis of the origins and history of the Weimar Republic remains the most profound and perceptive study so far, but on this point Rosenberg is wrong. The masses did not rebel against the Government. Strange though it may sound – they rebelled *for* the Government.

The earthquake of the second week of November began, as is well known, with a mutiny among the sailors of the High Sea Fleet against the Naval Command, but what triggered off this mutiny – a fact which has since been consistently glossed over – was another mutiny; a mutiny of the Naval Command against the Government and its policies.

When the ranks rose against this, they saw themselves as acting on the Government's behalf. The dramatic test of strength between sailors and naval officers which took place on October 30, 1918 on Schillig Wharf outside Wilhelmshaven and which started the Revolution, was not a test of strength between Government and Revolution. It was the first contest between the counter-Revolution and Revolution – and the counter-Revolution made the opening move.

When, in line with Wilson's demands, the Reich Government, on October 20, ordered the cessation of the U-boat war, the Naval Command decided to pick this moment for a decisive engagement between the German and the British Navies. This decision was by its nature mutinous. It was taken behind the back of the new Government and kept strictly secret from it. It was unmistakably intended to thwart the Government's policies. It expressed the

Kameraden!

Willkommen in der Heimat!

Ein erneuertes, verjüngtes Deutschland begrüßt Euch.
Das morsche System des Militarismus ist zusammengebrochen.
Die veraltete Kastenregierung ist weggefegt für immer.

Als

freie Männer

betretet Ihr den heiligen Boden eines

freien Deutschlands!

Nehmt den ersten Gruß des neuen Vaterlandes an seine tapferen Söhne!

Dank für Eure Taten! Dank für Eure Ausdauer!

Hört zugleich die Stimme der Heimat!

Sorgt alle dafür, daß das freie Deutschland nicht
abermals geknechtet werde! ━━━━━━━
Tod der Anarchie!   **Tod dem Chaos!**

Haltet Ordnung!

Sichert den ruhigen Verlauf der Demobilisation!
An ihr hängt alles!

Nur durch Ordnung erhalten wir
Freiheit, Frieden und Brot

Seid willkommen!

*Leaflet issued to Workers' and Soldiers' Councils and addressed to soldiers
returning from the front.*

unspoken and perhaps only half-conscious but unmistakable wish to ignore the 'Revolution from above' which had placed this Government of Parliamentary 'lily-livered pictures of misery' at the helm, to treat it as if it had not happened, if not to unmake it.

The attempt was later made to play down this decision to send out the entire German Fleet as a mere support operation to relieve pressure on the Army, a routine military operation of which the Government did not need to be informed. This is an untenable alibi and excuse. The battle on land in the west, with its critical points far inland, could not be decisively influenced at sea. No-one had ever thought this possible; the High Command had never demanded naval support for the land Army simply because such support would not have made military sense. If for the first time in two years the German Fleet was now to set sail in full array, this could have only *one* meaning, the same as in May 1916 at Jutland: to challenge the British Navy to a decisive naval battle.

Such a naval battle could no longer turn the fortunes of war, not even in the unlikely event of a victory over the British Navy, for the British Navy was now backed up by the American Fleet which could go on enforcing the blockade, and in any case, now that the War was about to be decided on land, the blockade no longer influenced the issue. But the terrible sacrifices of a great naval battle, irrespective of how it ended, were bound to rouse the enemy's fury and determination to a new white heat and destroy all hopes of an early and acceptable armistice such as the German Government was urgently working for. Now, more than ever, the decision to fight a naval battle was a highly political decision, and what is more, one which flew directly in the face of the Government. When the Naval Command took this decision completely on its own initiative, this was a major breach of discipline, insubordination, officers' mutiny. This officers' mutiny now provoked a mutiny in the ranks.

*

Discontent had long been smouldering among the ratings of the German Fleet. Breaches of discipline with political overtones had occurred in 1917 and had been suppressed with adamantine ruthlessness and punished with the utmost severity. But nothing of the sort had happened since and there is not the slightest shred of evidence that the disheartened sailors, with the longed-for end of the War in immediate reach, now intended off their own bat to risk their lives in a large-scale last-minute mutiny. However, they felt the same about a major naval battle. Now suddenly faced with the choice of once more risking their lives in one way or the other, the crews of several large ships (yet by no means all) opted for mutiny. Assuredly not from cowardice – mutiny in time of war requires more personal courage than battle – but because they felt themselves to be in the right.

On the *Thüringen*, one of the two ships of the line which on October 30 refused to sail, the sailors had a few days earlier sent a delegate to the First Officer and told him that the planned naval operation did not appear to fit in with the ideas of the new Government. According to the sailors' subsequent evidence before the court martial, the First Officer replied bitterly: 'Yes, there is *your* Government for you!' An exchange which reveals in a sudden flash the true confrontation. It was the officers who no longer acknowledged the Government as theirs; the crews who felt driven to fight for 'their' Government. In their view they were engaged in legitimate national self-defence and were defending overriding principles: their mutiny was against mutineers.

For days no one in Berlin or at Headquarters in Spa knew anything of the mutiny on Schillig Wharf. Kept secret, it ended in a draw. After breathtaking minutes during which the ships in mutiny and those which had not yet mutinied aimed their giant guns at each other from the closest proximity, the mutineers surrendered. Thus far the officers had won. But the naval engagement was abandoned: the Admirals felt they could not risk battle with so unreliable a crew. Thus far the crews had won. The fleet which had been assembled at Schillig Wharf was dispersed again. Only one squadron remained outside Wilhelmshaven, another was ordered to Brunsbüttel; the Third Squadron which had not mutinied steamed back to Kiel where it arrived on Friday, November 1. Over one thousand sailors were arrested and taken ashore into military prisons. They faced court martial and the execution squad.

Their fate was now at issue. The crews of the Third Squadron rode back to Kiel as gloomily as a week earlier they had set out for Wilhelmshaven. The 'death ride' which they then thought themselves to be heading for had indeed been thwarted. But now their comrades who had thwarted it were facing death. This thought gnawed at and fermented in the sailors. At Schillig Wharf only the crews of the *Thüringen* and of the *Helgoland* had in the end really mutinied, but almost all the others had been close to it, had merely lacked the courage to jump. Now this kept bothering them. Should their comrades on the *Thüringen* and the *Helgoland*, who had summoned enough courage and thus saved their lives, now die for it? They could not permit this. But if they were not to permit it, they now needed more than the courage they had failed to muster two days earlier at Schillig Wharf. For now they had to dare the unheard of, the unimaginable: no longer mere disobeying of orders but revolt, violence, seizure of power. And what would happen then? The prospect left them terrified. But to let their comrades die? Just as impossible, no, even more so.

It took three days before these men who had lacked the courage to mutiny in Wilhelmshaven found the courage to revolt in Kiel. On the first day they sent a delegation to the local commander to demand the release of the arrestees; it was of course refused. On the second day they spent hours in the trade union building at Kiel debating with marines and dockers what was to be done – and came to no conclusion. On the third day, Sunday November 3, they wanted to continue the discussions but found the union building locked and under armed guard. They therefore assembled in the open on a parade ground where they were joined by thousands of workers, listened to speeches and finally formed a great protest march. Some were armed. At a crossroads the march was stopped by a patrol. Its leader, a Lieutenant Steinhäuser, commanded: 'Disperse!' Then, when this did not happen: 'Fire!' Nine dead and twenty-nine injured were left lying in the road. The march scattered – but an armed sailor rushed forward and shot Lieutenant Steinhäuser dead.

And that was the moment of truth, the starting gun of the German Revolution had been fired. Suddenly all realized that now there was no backing out, and suddenly all knew what was to be done. On the morning of Monday, November 4, all the sailors of the Third Squadron elected Soldiers' Councils, disarmed their officers, armed themselves and ran up the red flag on their ships. One solitary ship, the *Schlesien*, did not take part: she ran out to sea under the threatening guns of her sister ships. Only one Captain, Captain Weniger of the *König*, drew his sword to protect his flag mast. He was shot dead.

Armed sailors, now under the command of their soldiers' councils, where a certain Able Seaman Artelt had grasped leadership, marched ashore in military formation, occupied the military prison without resistance and freed their comrades. Others occupied public buildings, yet others the railway station. The General Command at Altona had been asked for a detachment of soldiers to put down the sailors' revolt. They arrived at the station in the afternoon and were disarmed amid scenes of fraternization. The Commander of the port, suddenly stripped of all power, received a delegation from the soldiers' council and capitulated, grinding his teeth. The marines of the garrison declared their solidarity with the sailors. The dockers moved for a general strike. By the evening of November 4 Kiel was in the hands of 40,000 rebellious sailors and marines.

*

The sailors had no idea what to do with their newly gained power. When on the evening of November 4 there arrived from Berlin two emissaries of the disturbed Berlin Government, the Social Democrat delegate Gustav Noske and Secretary of State Haussmann, of the Liberal Party, they were welcomed with jubilation and relief. Noske was immediately elected 'Governor' – one more proof that the rebels were rebelling not *against* but for the Government and saw themselves as acting on its behalf. But one thing they instinctively knew: now they had taken the first big step in Kiel, overthrown the local authorities and seized the town, the movement must not remain limited to Kiel. Otherwise Kiel would become a trap. They could only escape by advancing: now they would have to break out and carry the movement further or their effort would be as suicidal as had been a week earlier the success of the mutineers at the Schillig Wharf, hundreds of whom were still imprisoned in Wilhelmshaven and Brunsbüttel. They would have to be liberated and then what had happened in Kiel would have to happen everywhere, or they were all lost. As the mutiny had grown into a revolt, so now the revolt had to grow into a revolution. The rebels had to seize power everywhere in the country as they had done in Kiel if they were not to be encircled in Kiel, overcome and cruelly punished. They had to swarm out and carry revolution into the land. This they now did with a success entirely beyond their expectations.

Wherever the sailors went the soldiers from the garrisons and the workers from the factories joined them as if they had been waiting for them; there was almost no serious resistance anywhere; everywhere the existing order cracked like rotten wood. On November 5 the Revolution had gripped Lübeck and Brunsbüttelkoog, on the 6th Hamburg, Bremen and Wilhelmshaven, on the 7th Hanover, Oldenburg and Cologne; on the 8th it was in control of all major west German cities and in Leipzig and Magdeburg it had reached across the River Elbe. From the third day onwards it no longer took sailors to trigger off Revolution; it was spreading under its own impetus like a forest fire. As if by tacit agreement the pattern everywhere was the same: the garrisons elected soldiers' councils, the workers elected workers' councils, the military authorities capitulated, surrendered or fled, the civil authorities, scared and cowed, recognized the new sovereignty of the workers' and soldiers' councils. The picture was the same everywhere: great processions in the streets, great popular demonstrations in the market places, everywhere scenes of fraternization among men in blue jackets, men in field grey, and haggard civilians. First the political prisoners were set free everywhere and the prisons occupied, then the town halls, the stations, the General Commands, sometimes the newspaper offices.

Of course one must not picture the election of workers' and soldiers' councils as being like an orderly poll in peacetime. In the barracks the most popular or respected soldiers were often appointed by their comrades by acclamation. The election of workers' councils only rarely took place in the factories and then in much the same way; usually members of the local party committees of the two socialist parties – the SPD and the Independents – were nominated as 'workers' councillors' and their nomination confirmed by acclamation in mass gatherings, often in the open in some central square. Usually the workers' councils were drawn equally from both parties. The masses were evidently intent upon reuniting the two warring fraternal factions who had split in the course of the War. The general undisputed consensus was that they should together form the new Government of the Revolution.

There was little resistance, violence or bloodshed. These days of Revolution were marked by a feeling of stupefaction: the authorities were stupefied by their sudden and unheralded impotence, the revolutionaries stupefied by their sudden and unheralded power. Both sides moved as in a dream. For the one it was a nightmare, for the others one of those dreams in which one can suddenly fly. The Revolution was good-natured. There was no mob rule and no revolutionary justice. Many political prisoners were set free but no one was arrested. At the worst a particularly hated officer or sergeant might have got beaten up. The revolutionaries contented themselves with depriving officers of their insignia of rank – this was as much part of the revolutionary ritual as was running up the red flag. Many of the victims, however, felt this to be a mortal insult. It is of little avail to the victorious masses to be good-natured; what their vanquished masters could not forgive was their victory.

*

Those temporarily vanquished masters were later to write the history of the November Revolution. It is thus not surprising that German history books have little good to say of the events of the week from November 4–10, 1918. It is denied even the honourable name of 'Revolution': the story is one of disorder, collapse, mutiny, treason, mob rule, chaos. In fact what took place during this week was a genuine revolution. What had happened in

Wilhelmshaven on October 30 had only been a mutiny – disobeying the orders of authority without any plan or intention to overthrow this authority. The events in Kiel on November 4 were already more than mutiny, a revolt: there the sailors had overthrown authority – admittedly without any idea of what was to take its place. But what swept across Germany west of the Elbe between November 4 and 10 was a true revolution; that is to say the overthrow of the old régime and its replacement by a new one.

In this week western Germany changed from a military dictatorship to a Republic of Workers' Councils, the so-called *Räterepublik*. The rising masses did not create chaos, they created everywhere the rough-hewn but recognizable elements of a new order. They put an end to the General Commands, the military overlords who had ruled every German town and rural district throughout the war under the state of emergency. The new revolutionary authority of the workers' and soldiers' councils took their place. The civil administration remained untouched and went on working under the supervision and superior authority of the councils as it had worked during the war under the supervision and superior authority of the military. The revolution did not touch private property. In the factories everything stayed as it was. But the military authorities who had been all powerful until now were swept away, together with the monarchs in whose name they had ruled and the military authority of the officers in the army units; the soldiers' councils replaced them all. The Revolution was not socialist or communist. It was – with a sort of tacit matter-of-factness, almost incidentally – republican and pacifist; consciously and above all, it was anti-militarist. What it got rid of and replaced by instituting the Workers' and Soldiers' councils, was the disciplinary powers of the officer corps in Army and Navy and the dictatorial executive powers the military had wielded in the country since 1914.

The masses who in the Workers' and Soldiers' Councils had created a new organ of state leadership, were no Spartacists or Bolsheviks. They were Social Democrats. The members of the Spartacist Union, the predecessor of what was later the Communist Party, provided no leaders for the Revolution, not even 'ringleaders'. Most of them were imprisoned until the Revolution set them free – Rosa Luxemburg, for example, was throughout this entire week still in the Breslau town jail, burning with impatience. She was freed only on November 9 after years of imprisonment; and Karl Liebknecht, released from prison on October 23, was in Berlin and had to rely on the newspapers for details of what was happening in the country during that week of Revolution.

The Russian example may have had an encouraging influence from afar but there were no Russian emissaries to provide the Revolution with leadership. In fact, anywhere but in Munich, this Revolution had no leaders and no organization, no general staff and no plan of operation; it was the spontaneous creation of the masses, of the workers and the common soldiers. Therein lay its weakness, all too soon to become evident, but therein also lay its glory.

For this week of Revolution was not without glory – however one may feel about its aims. It was a massive outbreak that had the qualities of greatness and nobility which were manifest in its actions: courage, decisiveness, readiness for sacrifice, unanimity, ardour, initiative, even inspiration and instinctive purposefulness, all that which glorifies a revolution; and this among leaderless masses, German masses at that! The often repeated allegation that the Germans were incapable of a revolution – one knows Lenin's scoffing remark that German revolutionaries could not occupy a railway station unless the counter were open for the sale of platform tickets – finds its rebuttal in this November week during which the German masses occupied not only many stations, but other more important buildings. In one town after the other thousands of them not only risked their lives but ventured the leap into the unknown, untried, incalculable which takes more courage than merely putting one's life at risk – revolutionary, not merely soldierly courage. The revolutionary achievement of the German masses in this week in November can stand comparison with their achievements as soldiers in the previous four years of War and does not fall short of the revolutionary achievement of the Russian masses in the March revolution of 1917. The ardour and impetus of this week even gripped people of the middle classes.

Rainer Maria Rilke, for example, who was hardly a revolutionary, was in fact something of a snob, wrote to his wife on November 7 after a revolutionary meeting in Munich:

... although you sat round the beer-tables and between the tables in such a way that the waitresses could only eat through the dense human structure like weevils – it was not in the least oppressive, not even for the breath; the fog of beer and smoke and people did not strike you as uncomfortable, you barely noticed it, so important was it and so clear above everything else that things could be said whose turn had at last come, and that the simplest and truest of these things, in so far as they were presented more or less intelligibly, were seized upon by the immense crowd with heavy and massive applause. Suddenly a pale young worker rose up, spoke quite simply: 'Have you or you or you, have any of you,' he said, 'made the offer of an armistice? And yet *we* are the people who ought to have done it, not these gentlemen at the top; if we could get hold of a radio station and speak as common people to the common people over there, Peace would come at once.' I cannot say it half as well as he did, but suddenly, when he had said this, a difficulty struck him, and with a touching gesture towards Weber, Quidde and the other professors standing on the stage beside him, he continued: 'Here, these professor chaps, they can speak French, they'll help us to say it properly, as we mean it . . .' Such moments are wonderful, there have been all too few of them here in Germany . . .

This eye-witness account is important not only because it catches, with a poet's sensibility, the atmosphere of this German Revolution, the peculiar mixture of grave courage and touching awkwardness, but also because, without the writer realizing it, it makes clear the Revolution's attitude to the Government. The revolutionaries in Munich, like the mutineers of Schillig Wharf ten days earlier, were not arrayed *against* the new Government. On the contrary, they shared its aims, they thought it needed their help and assistance. Peace was not to be left in the hands of the 'gentlemen up there': the masses themselves desired to re-enact and bring to completion what they felt the new Government had started and got bogged down with. The 'Revolution from below' did not mean to undo the 'Revolution from above', but to supplement it, animate it, push it forward, finally give it life. What it opposed was not the new parliamentary Government but the military dictatorship still functioning as a counter-government with martial law, censorship and preventive custody. With unerring instinct the masses sensed that this military régime was as much opposed to the Revolution from above as to that from below, that in truth it wanted neither peace nor democracy, that at heart it was bitterly and irreconcilably counter-revolutionary, and that it would have to be swept aside together with all the instruments of its power, all its insignia and symbols, in order to make room for the new common ideal, the new peacetime people's state. The Social Democrat masses who had these ideas and who were making revolution, thought they were at one in this with their leaders. It was their tragedy that they were wrong.

*

In the week of revolution no one suspected the imminence of this tragedy; yet its first scene was already being enacted. While the Revolution was spreading like wildfire everywhere – the very night Rilke penned his deeply-moved report, it conquered Munich – it had already died down in the very place where it had started: in Kiel. On the evening of Revolution Monday the SPD delegate Gustav Noske had arrived there to be jubilantly greeted by the sailors as 'their man' – the very next evening he phoned Berlin that he 'had but one hope: a voluntary return to order under Social Democrat leadership; then the rebellion would collapse' . . . On all sides, he reported, he noticed the inborn German feeling for order reawakening among workers and sailors. Reich Chancellor Prince Max von Baden, who made a note of it, on the same day got Cabinet approval for the decision: 'A free hand for Noske in his attempt to stifle the local outbreak.' And a few days later he was able to note to his satisfaction that Noske in Kiel had in the name of the revolution successfully called off the revolution, had re-established the authority of the humiliated officers, had even reinstated ships' patrols. Those sailors left in Kiel had returned to their normal duties. 'They don't want the English here', a satisfied

Noske told Berlin by telephone, and Prince Max was full of admiration for what Noske had accomplished in Kiel: 'The man has done superhuman work.' In his memoirs he later set down what he was already then beginning to suspect: 'Germany's fate depended on Ebert's repeating the role of his comrade on a large scale – by "rolling back" the movement in the country as a whole.'

Rolling back the movement – that, during Revolution week, was the only preoccupation of the three centres of power left in Germany, all of which were feeling the earth tremble under their feet: the Kaiser, and the High Command headed by Hindenburg and Groener at Spa in Belgium; the Reich Government headed by Prince Max von Baden in Berlin; and, also in Berlin, the Social Democrat Party leadership headed by Ebert who were carrying and supporting this Government but were now with forebodings seeing the hour approaching when they would have to step into the limelight and take office themselves to save the State. All three were agreed that the Revolution would have to be 'stifled' or 'rolled back'. As the days advanced it became their overriding concern. They were also agreed that an immediate armistice was the first priority; as long as the War continued, the Revolution would continue too.

There was, therefore, a deep sigh of relief both in Spa and in Berlin when on Wednesday morning, November 6, they heard from President Wilson that the allied Commander-in-Chief, General Foch, was now ready to receive the German armistice delegation at his Headquarters in Compiègne. That very day Secretary of State Erzberger got his marching orders, very much against his will, via Spa to Compiègne. (To the last moment the Government clung to the fiction that it had originated the request for an armistice, not the High Command; hence the highly unusual step of entrusting leadership of the delegation to a civilian politician, not to a general.) On Friday, November 8, at 10 a.m., Erzberger, together with the military retinue he had picked up in Spa on the way, stood in Compiègne facing Foch, who received him with the words: 'What brings the gentlemen hither? What do you want from me?' Told that they were seeking proposals for an armistice, he replied drily: 'I have no proposals to make.' In fact he made no 'proposals'. Instead he submitted a list of armistice conditions which had resulted from ten days of negotiations between the Allied governments, and an ultimatum to accept or reject these conditions within seventy-two hours. It was already clear that the ultimatum would be accepted.

*

But what would happen after the Armistice? Here the threatened overlords parted company. They were all agreed – Kaiser, High Command, Chancellor and SPD Leadership – that the most urgent task was to bring the Revolution to a halt and to rescue what was left of the existing state. They were also agreed that the Western Army would be the decisive factor, the only instrument of power that was still obedient, was not yet involved in the Revolution and was by the Armistice made available for use at home. But for whom or to what purpose the Western Army would be used – on this subject thoughts differed.

The Kaiser was convinced that under his leadership as supreme Warlord the Western Army would fight the 'inner enemy' as readily as the enemy outside, and he was determined to have it about-turn after the Armistice and march against its rebellious homeland.

General Groener and the Reich Chancellor Prince Max did not share this conviction. Both were secretly of the opinion that the Kaiser himself had become a bone of contention and would have to be removed if the Army were to remain under the control of its officers and put into action against the Revolution. The solution favoured by Prince Max was a personal abdication and the installation of a Viceroy or a Regent; General Groener felt the Kaiser should now seek death in battle. Neither dared to put their views to the Kaiser in person. They discussed them with their Cabinet colleagues or with other Generals; not with the Kaiser. The Cabinet colleagues glumly agreed or shrank back in horror. They too had no wish to speak to the Kaiser. So the days passed and nothing happened.

It was the SPD leaders who finally forced something to happen,

Der Rat der Volksbeauftragten

The Council of People's Representatives: (l to r) Dittmann (USPD), Landsberg (SPD), Haase (USPD), Ebert (SPD), Barth (USPD), Scheidemann (SPD). (*Photo: Staatsbibliotek, Berlin*)

Soldiers with flame-throwers and armoured cars during the street fighting in Berlin in March 1919. (*Photo: Staatsbibliotek, Berlin*)

particularly their Chairman, Friedrich Ebert, who day by day edged closer to the forefront of events. He was no opponent of the Government to which he had helped give birth and which he had supported from the first moment of its existence, no opponent in principle of the monarchy; in no way an opponent of the existing political order – he saw himself and his Party as preservers of the state, as its last reserve of strength; just like Groener and Prince Max he was concerned with saving the state and intercepting the Revolution. But he saw more clearly than Groener or Prince Max how strong the Revolution had already become and that not a single day must be wasted if it was to be stopped. Moreover he had one additional worry: if they were merely wondering how to retain control of the Western Army, Ebert was also concerned with keeping control of the SPD. Day by day he saw its members and provincial officers take a left-turn into the Revolution.

On Wednesday, November 6, Ebert with his colleagues of the SPD Executive appeared in the Reich Chancellery where General Groener had also turned up, and demanded the Kaiser's abdication. It had become necessary 'if the masses were to be prevented from going over to the camp of the revolutionaries'. This was 'the last chance to save the monarchy'. Groener indignantly refused – the suggestion was 'completely out of the question' – whereupon Ebert declared dramatically: 'Then things must take their course. From now on our paths divide. Who knows whether we shall ever meet again.'

But if Groener was not yet ready to listen – the Chancellor had been convinced by Ebert. Prince Max asked him to come back the next morning, Thursday, November 7, for a conversation *tête-à-tête*. It took place in the autumnal garden of the Reich Chancellery where the two men paced up and down among the withered leaves of the old trees. Prince Max later made a verbatim record of the decisive moments of the conversation. He acquainted Ebert with his decision to travel himself to Headquarters and urge the Kaiser to abdicate. 'If I succeed in convincing the Kaiser, can I count on your support in fighting the social revolution?' Prince Max continues:

Ebert's answer was unhesitating and unequivocal: 'Unless the Kaiser

3

abdicates, the social revolution is inevitable. But I will have none of it, I hate it like sin.'

After the Kaiser's abdication he hoped to bring round the party and the masses to the side of the government. We touched on the question of the Regency. I named Prince Eitel Friedrich as the Regent for Prussia and the Empire indicated by the Constitution. Ebert declared on behalf of himself and his party that on these constitutional points no difficulties would be put in the government's way.

Then, in words which betrayed his emotions he wished me success for my journey.

Too late! The journey did not take place, and the pact between Prince Max and Ebert fell apart on the very same day; for in the course of the day it became clear that the Revolution was now reaching for Berlin and there was no longer time for journeys to Spa. The Independents, the left-wing competitors of the SPD, had arranged twenty-six meetings that evening in Berlin. The Government wanted to ban the meetings. The SPD on the other hand were convinced that a ban would trigger off revolution in the capital. Their plan was to take over the meetings and take the sting out of them. At 5 p.m. they faced the Government with a new ultimatum: permission to hold the meetings and the Kaiser's abdication by Friday afternoon. To the Chancellor's outraged expostulations Ebert replied: 'Tonight we must announce the ultimatum from every rostrum, otherwise we lose the whole lot to the Independents. The Kaiser must abdicate at once or we shall have the revolution.' Suddenly Prince Max and Ebert who after all had the same aim – to get rid of the Kaiser and stifle the Revolution – seemed to face each other like enemies.

In all the confusion, the panic of these last days of the *Kaiserreich* hid something deeper and unspoken. All the protagonists, Groener and Prince Max on one side, Ebert on the other, saw something coming towards them that filled them with horror. All three of them saw that they would have to become traitors if they were to achieve their common aim: saving the existing state and the existing social order. Groener and Prince Max would have to betray their Imperial master to whom they had sworn allegiance.

Ebert would have to betray the Revolution which unsuspectingly offered him its leadership. Each of the three still hoped that the treason of one of the others would save him from having to turn traitor. Beneath the audible dialogue between them there ran another, subterranean, silent dialogue which went like this: 'If you betray the Kaiser I shall not have to betray the revolution.' – 'No, you pretend to take over the revolution and betray it, then we shall not have to betray the Kaiser.' But none of them would listen to the others' secret cry of distress and meanwhile the days passed and the sands of time ran out.

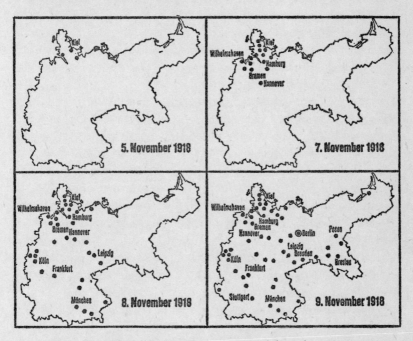

In the course of five days the Revolution spread throughout Germany.

In the end none of the three men were spared the great betrayal each had tried to push on to another. The moment of truth came on the same day, on Saturday, November 9. For the German monarchy and for the German Revolution alike this was the fateful day. It was the day on which the Kaiser fell by the hand of his paladins. It was also the day when the Revolution installed the man who was determined to stifle it.

5. November 9

On Friday evening, November 8, Herr Drews, the Prussian Minister of the Interior, drew out his watch at a meeting of the Cabinet and remarked: 'It is now 9.30, let us adjourn the meeting. Tomorrow there will be a general strike and bloody riots are likely. Everything depends on whether the Army stands fast or not. If not, then tomorrow there will be no Prussian Government.' War Minister von Scheüch took umbrage: 'What makes Your Excellency think that the Army will not stand fast?'

At about the same time Richard Müller, leader of an illegal group of conspirators who had for days been planning a *coup* for the following Monday, stood by the Halle Gate in Berlin. 'Heavily armed columns of infantry, machine-gun companies and light field artillery moved past me in an endless stream towards the heart of the city. The troopers looked pretty tough. I felt uneasy.' What frightened Müller and gave von Scheüch his confidence was the Fourth Regiment of Fusiliers, a unit regarded as particularly reliable, which during the summer had several times been successfully sent into action in the East against Russian revolutionaries. Now they were to be sent into action in Berlin against German revolutionaries. They had got their marching orders the previous day in Naumburg to reinforce the Berlin Garrison. Late at night on November 8 they moved into the Alexander Barracks. That very night hand grenades were distributed. This led to an incident.

A lance-corporal made a rebellious remark. He was immediately arrested and taken away, without resisting. But suddenly, after the event, the men, to the dismay of their officers, began to grumble and to ask questions aloud. Even these 'tough troopers' were suddenly heard to say strange things. What was it all about? What were they doing here in Berlin? Wasn't everyone talking about the end of the War and the Kaiser's abdication? Hadn't they got Social Democrats in the Government? Could they really be meant to fight against the Government? They no longer understood anything. Before they threw hand grenades at German compatriots, they wanted to know exactly what was up. The officers managed to calm them down somewhat by promising them that everything would be made perfectly clear to them the next morning. So the men first of all went to bed. After all they were tired; they had had a long day's march. But on Saturday morning, after reveille, they agreed quite suddenly to find out for themselves. A delegation went by lorry to the offices of the SPD newspaper *Vorwärts*. It is not clear whether the officers were informed of this and had given their agreement.

At *Vorwärts* the SPD shop stewards had been in session since 7 a.m. They were waiting for news of whether the Kaiser had abdicated or whether 'things would start'. They were waiting impatiently. They were no longer sure of their influence in the factories. More radical men than they were now being listened to there. If something didn't happen soon 'things might start' without them. The soldiers broke into this nervous gathering. Had they perhaps come to arrest them? Anything was possible. There they stood by the door, self-assured, demanding. Someone was to come with them, immediately, to put the unit in the picture. What could this mean? The SPD delegate Otto Wels decided to risk the journey into the lion's den; he was a stocky, powerful man and a genial soul. He travelled in the lorry with the soldiers, a lonely civilian surrounded by heavily armed men. He had no idea what awaited him.

In the square of the Alexander Barracks the entire unit had formed up in military order, with the officers in front. Wels did not know their mood. Hauled on top of a regimental dog-cart he began to speak. He began carefully, being neither provocative nor inflammatory. He spoke sadly and simply of the War that had been lost, of President Wilson's hard conditions, of the Kaiser's obstinacy, of the hope for peace. While speaking he slowly began to sense agreement among the men, uncertainty among the officers. Slowly he felt his way forward, became more explicit –

until he risked it: 'It is our duty to prevent civil war! I call upon you to cheer the peoples' free state!' And suddenly a roar – he had won.

The ranks rushed forward and surrounded the cart on which he stood erect, an easy target if someone had wanted to shoot. But no officer fired. Wels returned in triumph with sixty men who were to protect *Vorwärts* – and then went on to the other barracks of the Berlin garrison. He now knew what mattered and how he had to handle the soldiers. The Naumburg Fusiliers had given him his clue.

It was 9 a.m., Berlin was still quiet, the workers were still in their factories. In the capital the Revolution had not yet begun – but its fate was sealed in advance. Armed power in Berlin was now in the hands of the SPD. On this day it meant the end of the *Kaiserreich*. By the next day it was to mean the end of the Revolution.

In the very hour when Wels returned to *Vorwärts* with his military escort, at Headquarters in Spa, Hindenburg and Groener went to the Kaiser to inform him that he no longer had the backing of the field Army. The previous evening – at about the time when the Prussian Minister of the Interior said prophetically: 'Everything depends on whether the Army stands fast' – they had received shattering news: the Second Division of Guards, made up of the Prussian King's Own Regiments, had been ordered back from the front to Aix-la-Chapelle in order to retake Cologne from the revolutionaries and thereby secure the most important line of supply and retreat for the army. But they had 'broken their allegiance to their officers and against their express orders had set off to march home'. The Second Division of Guards! If *it* could not be relied on, that was the end.

On the same morning thirty-nine unit commanders had arrived from the front with instructions to report whether their units were ready to fight for the Kaiser against the Revolution. Before calling on the Kaiser and leaving the officers with the Chief of Operations, Colonel Heye, for more detailed interrogation, Hindenburg and Groener briefly listened to them. Their verdict confirmed the experience with the Second Division of Guards:

the units could no longer be used for action in a civil war. The day before at the morning audience the Kaiser had announced his intention to place himself at the head of his Army immediately after the Armistice and restore order at home, and had given General Groener the formal order to prepare this operation. Now Groener had to explain to him that the order could not be executed. He did this at length, drily and unemotionally, with much technical detail. His report culminated in the sentence: 'The Army will march back to the homeland in closed ranks and good order under its leaders and commanding generals, but not under the leadership of Your Majesty.' The much-quoted sentence: 'The oath of loyalty is now a mere notion' was not spoken during this conversation. Groener did not address it to the Kaiser but said it later in conversation with other officers. Shortly afterwards Colonel Heye, who had since individually sounded out the thirty-nine commanding officers, confirmed it to the Kaiser: 'The Army will march home under the sole leadership of its generals. If Your Majesty should march with it, it will not mind and will be pleased. But one thing the Army no longer wants is to fight, either abroad or at home.'

So in Spa, too, the hour had struck: like the Berlin garrison the Army in the field could no longer be used to put down the Revolution. The *Kaiserreich* had no means left to defend its existence, either at the Front or at home.

*

On the morning when news of the defection of the Army reached the Chancellery, Prince Max von Baden realized (as he later noted) that: 'We can no longer suppress the Revolution by force, we can only stifle it.' General Groener probably had similar thoughts at this time. Stifling the Revolution – that meant handing it an illusory victory on a plate, evacuating advanced positions for it to occupy, in order to bring it to a halt from carefully prepared positions in the rear. In factual terms: the Kaiser had to abdicate, the semi-Social Democrat Government would have to go entirely Social Democrat and Friedrich Ebert would have to become Reich Chancellor. It was then up to Ebert to get rid of an apparently victorious Revolution still reeling from the surprise of its own all-too-easy victory and to restore order. In the words of Prince Max: 'to do in the country as a whole what Noske had already done in miniature in Kiel'. It was a role Ebert was perfectly willing to play, and Prince Max knew this; General Groener at least suspected it. From early on November 9, if not sooner, these three men were pulling in the same direction. They were all acting in line with the same plan.

But not to the same timetable – and that led to the drama of November 9, a drama which for all its pathos and suspense, was not without moments of comedy. On that morning Groener thought that he still had a few days' grace before the Armistice; Prince Max thought he had at least a few hours – Berlin still seemed quiet. But Ebert had not a minute to lose: during the morning-break, factory workers everywhere were gathering and forming columns. If the SPD did not join these marchers at once and appear to take the lead, it would lose control. The result was that Ebert had to act without being able to wait for Prince Max, and that Prince Max had to act without being able to wait for Groener; that in Spa they spent the whole day performing a drama of abdication which had long been overtaken by the events in Berlin; that Prince Max after hours of anguish announced the Kaiser's abdication without it having taken place; and that even this misrepresentation came too late to stop the course of events.

Almost everything which, on this day, had the remaining dignitaries of the *Kaiserreich* in a state of excitement and high tension was, in reality, no longer of any importance. In Spa and in the Chancellery they were performing the last act of the *Kaiserreich* with heightened pathos – and total irrelevance. They were like actors in a historical drama rolling their eyes and declaiming their lines in a fine frenzy when the curtain has already dropped.

Shortly after 9 a.m. Spa phoned the Chancellery (using a secret direct line which was later to play an important part) to say that the High Command was now ready to inform the Kaiser that he had lost the Army's backing. The Chancellery at once phoned this news to Ebert: 'Revolution superfluous, abdication imminent.' Ebert replied: 'Too late! The ball has been set rolling. One factory is already in the streets.' After a short pause he added. 'We shall see what can be done.'

But if for Ebert – much to his regret – it was already too late, in Spa it was still much too soon for final decisions. Admittedly at about 11 a.m. the Kaiser, in a private conversation with one of his personal advisers, for the first time talked openly of abdicating, in a disgruntled and disparaging tone: 'I have reigned long enough to know what an ungrateful business it is. I am far from wanting to cling to it.' But that was far from being a firm decision, and in the next hour the Kaiser suddenly indulged in a new idea: to divest himself of the mantle of Emperor, but to remain King of Prussia. At twelve the Crown Prince arrived, naïve and forthright as ever: 'Have those piffling sailors not been put to the wall yet?' Father and son had their discussion in the park. No one heard them talking; everything was again in doubt. Meanwhile a succession of urgent phone calls from Berlin: the abdication would have to be announced at once if it was still to make an impact, every minute counted. Spa made the pained reply that such important decisions could not be unduly hurried. His Majesty had made his decision but it still had to be formulated and would Berlin kindly be patient.

At noon, with news reaching the Chancellery of huge columns of workers pouring towards the city centre from the factory estates, the Chancellor finally lost his patience. The official announcement of the Kaiser's abdication had been prepared hours ago, at his instruction. Now he ordered it to be made public, knowing full well that it was premature. The official news agency issued this statement:

The Emperor and King has decided to renounce the throne. The Reich Chancellor will remain in office until the problems connected with the Kaiser's abdication, the renunciation of the throne by the Crown Prince of the German Reich and of Prussia and the installation of the Regency have been settled. He intends to propose to the Regent that Representative Ebert be appointed Reich Chancellor and a bill be drafted for the holding of immediate general elections for a German National

Constituent Assembly which would have the task of giving final form to the future Constitution of the German people, inclusive of those parts of the people who might wish to come within the frontiers of the Reich.

In anticipating the Kaiser's decision and telling the people of an abdication that had not yet happened, Prince Max felt he was committing a terrible deed. He had hesitated for many agonizing hours before summoning enough courage, and in fact for a man of his background and position it would have been a classical piece of villainy – if it had still had the least significance. But it signified nothing. The princely Chancellor's gesture resembled the gesture of a circus clown who pretends to be directing the show; it was pure comedy, no less so than the comedy about the order to fire which followed hard upon it. The Commanding Officer of Berlin, General von Linsingen, enquired whether there was any point in using firearms in view of the fact that the majority of the troops would not fire in any case. After hasty consultation with his staff the Chancellor brought himself to reply: 'Only to protect the lives of citizens and to protect Government buildings.' This answer was lost in the void, for Linsingen, under pressure of time and circumstances, had himself already issued the order: 'Troops are not to use arms, not even in defence of buildings.' And even that came too late, for by the time the order reached them, the soldiers were already fraternizing cheerfully with the approaching workers and would not have fired in any event.

Meanwhile, a few minutes after noon, Ebert had turned up in the Chancellery with a delegation of the SPD Executive and demanded that he and his Party take over the Government 'to preserve law and order'. The announcement that the Chancellor was to stay in office until the question of the Regency was settled had only just been issued but the Prince did not resist. Basically he and Ebert wanted the same thing, and he was immensely relieved that Ebert was now ready to rid him of all further responsibilities. He therefore ceded to him the Chancellorship: as yet the Chancellorship of the Imperial Government – just after having, however prematurely, announced the Kaiser's abdication. Even if he had not done that, the transfer would still have been constitutionally impossible – no Chancellor has the right to nominate another. But whatever the rights or wrongs, the Government Ebert now took over was still the old Government; all Secretaries of State remained in office, even the Prussian War Minister, von Scheüch; the only difference was that the Chancellor was now called Friedrich Ebert instead of Max von Baden. His first act in office was a proclamation to the marching workers of Berlin: 'Fellow citizens! With the agreement of all Secretaries of State the present Reich Chancellor has entrusted me with the conduct of the business of the Reich Chancellor . . . Fellow citizens! I urge all of you: Leave the streets! Preserve law and order!' But Ebert was too late. The call to leave the streets was lost in the void like Prince Max's premature announcement of the Kaiser's abdication and his half-hearted order to fire. The masses were in the streets in their hundreds of thousands and had – one o'clock was approaching – reached the city centre. The leaflets with Ebert's proclamation were discarded unread.

*

The next great scenes of this free-wheeling tragi-comedy took place over lunch. There were three of them.

The first was played in the Reichstag where Ebert and Scheidemann were lunching on the watery potato soup that was on the menu, sitting at separate tables. The two leaders of the SPD did not particularly like each other. As they were eating, there was a noise outside; a huge swarm of people had reached the Reichstag, they were shouting for Ebert and Scheidemann, punctuated with rhythmic chants of 'Down with the Kaiser, down with the War!' and 'Up the Republic!' Representatives came rushing in begging Ebert and Scheidemann to address the crowds. Ebert shook his head and went on eating his soup. But Scheidemann, who was a brilliant orator and somewhat proud of it, left his soup and hurried through the long ornate corridors of the Reichstag. In passing, he overheard with silent amusement a group of Representatives and senior officials discuss the selection of a Regent. He reached a window and opened it. Below he saw the gigantic crowd fall silent at the sight of him, the forest of red flags, thousands of emaciated, careworn, devout faces looking up at him ecstatically. What a moment! This was his hour, stirring off-the-cuff speeches were his *forte*; he found his tongue, the words came in a rush. 'The people have won all along the line!' he shouted, and then, into the mounting roar of delight: 'Long live the German Republic!'

He himself thought he had not done too badly and, pleased with himself, went back to the dining-room where his watery soup had grown cold. But suddenly Ebert stood at his table, his face livid with rage: 'He banged his fist on the table and yelled at me: "Is it true?" When I told him that it was not only true but a matter of course he made a scene which took me completely aback. "You have no right to proclaim the Republic. What is to become of Germany, a Republic or whatever, will be decided by a Constituent Assembly!" ' Thus wrote Scheidemann in his *Memoirs of a Social Democrat*.

In fact Ebert himself was not about to leave everything to a Constituent Assembly. When Prince Max came a few hours later to take his leave, he asked him to stay on – as Administrator of the Reich. He was as ready as Scheidemann to do the Assembly's job for it – only in the reverse sense; he did not want a republic, he wanted to save the monarchy, even now. But Prince Max was no longer inclined to play a part, he had packed his bags. That very afternoon he departed; home to South Germany, making his exit from seething, turbulent Berlin – and from history.

*

While Ebert and Scheidemann were eating in the Reichstag, in Spa the Kaiser was taking his meal in the royal train. He was at table when they brought him the news just received by telephone from Berlin – the news that Prince Max had announced His Majesty's abdication. The Kaiser was professionally trained to self-control. He went on eating mechanically. Then he slowly turned pale and began: 'That a Prince von Baden should overthrow the King of Prussia . . .' he did not finish the sentence. His voice broke.

He had just signed the document in which he abdicated as

Emperor but not as King of Prussia, and was engaged in inwardly rehearsing his new role as King of Prussia. And now this! After the meal, at coffee with a small private entourage, his indignation exploded: 'Treason, shameless outrageous treason!', he kept repeating loudly and filled hurriedly-ordered telegram forms with increasingly sharply worded messages of protest. None of them were sent. And the addressee was no longer there to receive them.

In the Reich Chancellery in Berlin the mid-day meal was also interrupted, by a telephone call reporting the partial abdication – as Emperor, but not as King of Prussia – and they were hardly less indignant about this than the Kaiser was about the conduct of Prince Max. 'What are you saying?' Under-Secretary of State Wahnschaffe shouted into the instrument, 'Abdicate as Emperor but not as King of Prussia? But that is of absolutely no use to us, that is constitutionally quite impossible!' The constitutional impossibility was largely irrelevant – everything that had happened in the last few hours was constitutionally impossible. The gentlemen at the Chancellery were much more indignant at not having been consulted about such a plan, and in this they were quite right. The whole thing had been dreamt up on the spur of the moment. Berlin accordingly completely ignored it. The information was filed in the archives and never made public. The Kaiser's partial abdication never took effect.

In fact the Kaiser did not abdicate on November 9, 1918 (he did it three weeks later in Holland) and, as yet, Germany was no republic. That Scheidemann had cheered the republic from a Reichstag window was constitutionally irrelevant. Prince Max's abdication announcement had simply been a false report. The declaration by which the Kaiser withdrew to the status of King of Prussia remained an invalid draft buried without countersignature in the Chancellery archives. And the man who had now become Reich Chancellor, even if in a highly irregular manner, still considered himself an Imperial Chancellor and still strove to save the monarchy somehow. But the monarchy was beyond salvation. In German minds, including those of monarchists, it ended on that day, and the Kaiser himself finally gave it the *coup de grâce*, not by abdicating (this was no longer on the agenda) but by slipping out of the country.

*

It is not clear who first suggested his departure. It was not an obvious solution. The Kaiser was in no personal danger. In Spa he moved between his residence, the Headquarters and the royal train without interference, the guards as always presenting arms. There was no revolution in Spa. The unit Commanders had told Colonel Heye only a few hours earlier that the troops would not mind and would 'be pleased' if the Kaiser were to join them on a peaceful march home. And yet after lunch everyone was suddenly talking about the safety of the Kaiser's person and the question of where he would live in future. All seemed agreed that the Kaiser was in danger and that he would have to leave. Only Groener disagreed: 'I would point out that when the Kaiser has abdicated he can go where he likes. Until he has abdicated he must not abandon the Army. To abandon the Army without abdicating is an impossibility.'

Embarrassed silence greeted this remark. Nobody seemed to want to understand. After a short pause the discussion about possible itineraries continued as if Groener had not spoken. Even Hindenburg, who had been very reserved throughout the day, said repeatedly: 'In an extreme emergency crossing the frontier to Holland might be considered.' The court officials put forward the thought that if the Kaiser intended to travel, the decision would have to be taken soon, so that the Dutch Government might be advised. Although no definite decision had actually been taken, everyone was soon busy telephoning. At five o'clock the Kaiser, who had not been present, suddenly summoned the Chiefs of Command to say goodbye. He refused to shake General Groener's hand: 'Now that I have resigned the High Command I have no longer anything to do with you. You are a General from Württemberg.' Evidently he somehow viewed Groener's request that he should remain with the Army as long as he had not abdicated, as a personal insult; evidently he also still considered himself King of Prussia. But the King of Prussia now abandoned the Army.

There was still some dithering. Suddenly the word went round: 'We are not going'; then again, 'We are going.' In the event the Kaiser, his luggage packed, spent the night in the royal train and, at 5 a.m. the next morning, the train steamed out of Spa Station in the direction of the Dutch border. Like Prince Max von Baden twelve hours earlier the Kaiser now made his exit from history, and the German monarchy exited with him. After this precipitate departure nothing could have saved it. It had not abdicated, it had wiped itself out.

The Kaiser's clandestine getaway and the soundless collapse of the German monarchy which it implied were of momentous importance for Germany's distant future. It deprived the German upper classes of their tradition and mainstay; it imparted to their imminent counter-Revolution a desperate and nihilist air which it would hardly have had as a movement to restore the monarchy; it left the vacuum that Hitler was ultimately to fill. But what the Kaiser did or did not do had become totally irrelevant to the immediate drama of November 9 and 10. Whether he abdicated or not, whether he stayed in Spa or went to Holland, could no longer have any effect on events in Berlin where since early on November 9 the workers had been on the move and the soldiers had joined the socialist camp. The defender of the old order was no longer the Kaiser, it was Ebert. And Ebert, on the afternoon of November 9, unlike Prince Max in the morning, had no time to worry about the Kaiser; he had quite different worries. For on this same afternoon the Revolution threatened to engulf Ebert as well.

6. Ebert's Hour

Friedrich Ebert who, on November 9, 1918, became Germany's man of destiny was not impressive to look at. He was a short, fat man, with short legs, a short neck, and a pear-shaped head on a pear-shaped body. And he was not a compelling orator. His voice was throaty when he read his speeches. He was not an intellectual yet not a man of the people. His father had been a master tailor (like the father of Walter Ulbricht) and he himself had been apprenticed to a saddler; since childhood horses had been his secret love. Later, as Reich President, he went for regular morning rides in the Tiergarten.

Ebert was a typical German artisan: solid, conscientious, a man of limited outlook but within his limitations a man of skill; quietly dignified in his treatment of important customers, laconic and bossy in his own workshop. The SPD officials tended to shake in their boots in his presence like journeymen or apprentices in the presence of a strict master. He was not particularly popular in the Party but he enjoyed enormous respect. He had played no big part in the great discussions which shook the Party before the War – about revolution or reform, mass action or parliamentarianism – but when he was elected to the Party Executive he had at once installed telephones and typewriters and a decent filing system in the Party offices. Ebert could be relied on to be systematic. When the War broke out he had been picked as the man to take the Party funds to Zurich where they would be out of harm's way. He was a man one could trust, a man who always knew what he wanted.

What did he want? Quite certainly not a revolution. He hated it 'like sin'. If he hated anything more, it was lack of discipline in his Party. 'It will lead to the collapse of the Party,' he had stated in 1916, 'if discipline and confidence are destroyed and all the foundations of the organization allowed to perish. This is the Party's great danger! We must put a stop to these goings-on.' In those days this had sufficed to split the Party. In 1917 all those restless spirits who could no longer bear to be under Ebert's thumb had finally split off and formed the Independent Social Democrat Party (USPD). Ebert looked upon this new Party of the Left not only with disfavour but also with contempt: a pigsty lacking all discipline and structure.

He wanted the best for his Party and he had not the least doubt what this best was: more power for the Reichstag, with the Reichstag franchise extended to Prussia; this would automatically take the SPD into the Government, perhaps even make it the strongest Party in the Government, and then it would be able to introduce social reforms and improve the workers' lot. Friedrich Ebert did not want more: that was the extent of his vision.

In the German Empire, as it then was, Ebert did not see much to find fault with. During the War he had of course been a patriot but he was not cast down by defeat: 'With calm and fortitude,' he told the Reichstag on October 22, 'we await the results of our peace initiative. We may lose our goods and chattels – but no one can take from us the strength to create anew. Whatever may happen, we remain at the heart of Europe as a numerous, capable, honour-loving people.'

Basically, Ebert by October 1918 had achieved everything he had ever striven for. He was more than happy that the Party found itself sharing power with respectable bourgeois partners and equally pleased that there was still a Kaiser awesomely brooding over the whole. That at this moment the Revolution had to break out! And that his own supporters were responsible! For Ebert this was a dreadful stroke of misfortune, a terrible misunderstanding. But he thought he was the man to cope with it.

He was now Reich Chancellor, backed by the State, by organized authority, by the Civil Service and by the Armed Services – or what was left of them. He embodied order. And surely that was what counted? Was an orderly Government not necessary to achieve the Armistice and peace that all were longing for? Was not order necessary if a catastrophic famine was to be avoided? Ebert *wanted* order. Ebert *was* order, and it seemed a safe bet to him that the Germans could rapidly be won back to their sense of order.

Moreover Ebert had another trump card up his sleeve: he was not only Chancellor, he was also Chairman of the SPD. He embodied not merely order as such, he embodied the *new* order. The revolutionaries – who were largely Social Democrats themselves – whom would they want to place at the head of the Reich if not their own Party Chairman? Agreed, there were still those restless spirits of the USPD, there was still that awkward Karl Liebknecht who had now become so popular as a martyr of the protest against the War. Well, one would in God's name take a few USPD people into the Government and gag the Revolution that way. They would not be able to do too much damage. Before lunch on November 9 Ebert received a USPD delegation in the Chancellery and invited them to nominate three candidates for ministerial office. One of them asked if they could nominate whom they chose. 'Yes,' Ebert replied. 'We shall not let questions of personality stand in our way.' 'Liebknecht too?' the USPD man questioned. 'If you want to, bring in Karl Liebknecht,' was Ebert's reply, 'he will be welcome.'

Then they all went to the Reichstag, Ebert to eat his potato soup in silent isolation, the USPD emissaries to spend the whole afternoon arguing inconclusively with their Parliamentary Party about participating in the Government. They were after all an undisciplined lot where everyone held his own views. The Reichstag began to look like an Army camp that afternoon; the SPD and USPD Parliamentary Parties were in constant session and every now and again someone from the SPD poked his head through the USPD door to ask if they had at last reached a decision. Outsiders also joined the USPD meeting; at one point Karl Liebknecht turned up to enquire what it was all about and then 'in a triumphant, almost imperious tone' dictated to the Secretary the words: 'All executive, all legislative, all judiciary power to the workers' and soldiers' councils' – whereupon a passionate discussion at once flared up. But other gate-crashers also rushed into

the Reichstag – unknown, uninvited ones, at times entire processions waving red flags. There was a constant coming and going.
On that afternoon of November 9 the streets in the centre of
Berlin resembled a surging sea, and again and again a breaker from
this sea of people rolled into the Reichstag.

No one actually attempted to count the numbers that poured
into the city on November 9, but all eye-witnesses speak of
hundreds of thousands. They had all experienced a dramatic
change of mood. In the morning each and every one of them had
been prepared to march to their death. They had no idea that the
Army 'no longer stood fast', they expected machine-gun fire as
they arrived in front of barracks and Government buildings. As –
slowly and heavily – the endless columns approached from all
directions, the front ranks were carrying placards: 'Brothers, don't
shoot!' In the rear many carried arms. With grim determination
they were ready to fight to the death for the barracks. The day
was overcast and mild for the time of year, the air heavy, almost
sultry; a day pregnant with a sense of foreboding and ill omen, a
proper day for dying.

And then nothing happened! The 'brothers' in fact did not
shoot, they themselves threw open the barracks, they helped hoist
the red flags, they joined the masses or – like the police guards in
Police Headquarters in the Alexanderplatz – they unstrapped their
weapons and made off as quickly as they could! People were so
taken aback that they formed gangways to let the police go home
unmolested; no one even shouted insults. The Revolution in
Berlin was as good-natured as it had been everywhere else. The
other side were responsible for such bloodshed as there was: in the
Maikäfer Barracks a few officers suddenly fired when the door of a
room in which they had barricaded themselves was torn open.
Three people were killed; more died later during similar incidents
in the *Marstall* and in the university, fifteen all told. But in the
immensity of the crowds these deaths went unnoticed. Since noon,
when the fear and tension in the face of the expected massacre had
shown itself to be groundless, there was everywhere immense
relief, even a sense of deliverance and exaltation – and at the same
time a sense of anticlimax, and of perplexity. What now remained

to be done? All that was left, overflowing the streets, was an aimless throng, fraternizing in a mood of muted celebration – muted because there was nothing to celebrate; and the duped readiness to face death left a strangely empty feeling.

All the same, here and there courageous men with a gift for organization and improvisation took the initiative, assembled columns of armed men and trucks and got something done. First of all, as everywhere else, they occupied the prisons and set free the political prisoners – only the politicals, all properly and according to the files! Then they occupied the railway stations, the main post offices, also several newspaper offices (at *Vorwärts* the attempt was foiled by the Naumburg Fusiliers who had been standing guard there since morning). Unguarded Government buildings were left in peace; the word had gone around that these already contained a People's Government. But at 4 p.m. someone raised the cry: 'To the Palace!' Half an hour later the Royal Palace was occupied and Karl Liebknecht appeared on a balcony draped with a red blanket and for the second time that day proclaimed the Republic – this time the Socialist Republic. His solemn voice with its almost clerical chant rang out over the square where the crowds stood densely packed. He ended with these words: 'Those among you who want to see the Free Socialist Republic of Germany and world revolution come to pass, raise your hand and swear!' They all swore. Who knows how many kept the oath?

Karl Liebknecht's was a big name in those days, perhaps the biggest in Germany. Everyone knew of him and no one remained indifferent: he aroused the most intense love and the most fervid hatred. But he was a symbolic figure, not a powerful one. It was only two weeks since he had been released from the prison where he had spent the previous two and a half years as a result of his single-handed public protest against the War. He belonged to no party (the USPD had been formed when he was already in jail), he had no organization to back him and no gift for organization as the coming weeks were to show. He had played no part whatever in the revolutionary events of the past week; on this November day, the 9th, his was, as it were, merely a subsidiary decorative role in Berlin. He was not the leader of the Revolution.

His appearance on the Palace balcony was no more than a stirring interlude, an episode which had no effect on the course of events.

But there was another group of men who thought themselves equipped to grasp the leadership of the Revolution and whose intervention was to change the course of events of this eventful day in the most dramatic manner: they were the Revolutionary Shop Stewards (*Obleute*) of Berlin's great factories, a group of some hundred men, with a nucleus of about a dozen; genuine skilled workers and experienced workers' leaders whose names (unlike Liebknecht's) were unknown in Germany outside their factories, but who (again unlike Liebknecht) had the backing of an organization, namely the workers of their factories on whose allegiance they could count.

The group of Revolutionary Shop Stewards had been formed during the big strikes of the past winter. They had been the real strike leaders. Since then they had conspired together and for some weeks had been planning the Revolution. On November 4 – without the least inkling of the avalanche which started that day in Kiel – they had decided on a coup in Berlin planned for November 11. They had obtained and distributed arms and drafted plans for a surprise attack on the centres of Government. Events had then left the Shop Stewards behind, but they had no intention of letting themselves be passed over. On the afternoon of November 9 – while the masses, enthusiastic, aimless and already tiring, were surging through the streets of Berlin, while Ebert was attempting to govern in the Reich Chancellery, and while the SPD and the USPD were having their endless meetings in the Reichstag and failing to agree on the conditions for USPD participation in Ebert's Government – the Revolutionary Shop Stewards held a hurried consultation and then went into action.

They were no great theoreticians or planners, but men with practical ideas. They saw clearly what was now at issue: to provide the masses with a spearhead capable of action, an organ capable of political intervention, a revolutionary government which could push Ebert and the parties to one side. They drummed up a few hundred of their followers. In the evening as darkness fell and the masses in the streets slowly began to disperse, they occupied the Reichstag.

*

There had been wild, uncontrolled coming and going in the Reichstag all day. The group which suddenly pushed its way in between 8 and 9 p.m. had at first attracted no attention, particularly as it was as motley in its composition as were all the weird visitors the Reichstag had seen that day. Nobody was, after all, issuing entry tickets, and all manner of curious or enterprising people, in uniform or in civilian dress, had tagged along with the column of the Revolutionary Shop Stewards. But suddenly this column manifested something resembling planned action. The group, numbering several hundred men, began by occupying Room 17, then the main assembly chamber which they decorated with red sheets brought along for the purpose. Someone had taken the Chair, the President's bell was rung, the delegates' seats were taken, the turbulent gathering was brought to order, an Executive was proposed and elected. From outside the chamber one could hear speeches and applause, the whole ritual of a normal session of the Reichstag. The delegates who had been roused from their meeting rooms and who rushed up to see what was happening, were taken aback at being suddenly confronted with a revolutionary parliament in full progress.

It was a turbulent, random, unelected parliament but evidently one quite capable of functioning. A group of men occupying the Ministerial benches had the assembly pretty well in hand. They were the leaders of the Revolutionary Shop Stewards, a few of them familiar faces, such as Richard Müller and Emil Barth. They cut short wild speeches, gave each other the chance to speak, themselves spoke briefly and effectively, and evidently knew exactly what they wanted. Soon they were putting actual resolutions forward, and those assembled were actually voting on them. Shortly after 10 p.m. a few people from the SPD who had been listening left the hall in a hurry, covered the short distance from the Reichstag to the Chancellery in record time and, in dismay, reported to Ebert what had happened: an assembly in the Reichstag had just resolved that the following morning all factories and barracks should elect workers' and soldiers' councillors – one representative per battalion and per 1,000 workers – and that these elected councillors should meet at 5 p.m. in the Busch Circus to nominate a provisional government, a 'Council of People's Commissars'. There had been no mention of Ebert's Government; they had acted as if there was no Government left; they evidently intended simply to shoulder the Government aside. By now emissaries from the Reichstag were probably on their way to drum up workers and soldiers everywhere. The whole thing seemed to be a coup d'état by the *Obleute* of whose existence and power in the factories one had a rough idea.

Ebert listened to these ill tidings in grim silence, without visible excitement but with an ashen face and compressed lips. 'Alright,' he said, 'wait here in the ante-room.'

*

What Ebert had aimed at on this day is perfectly clear from everything he said and did – he wanted to stop the Revolution at the last moment, to arrange for the workers' great march to pass off as a mere demonstration, to save the essentials of the old order and to carry on business under a new letter-head. Prince Max's programme – the Kaiser's abdication, a Regency, an Armistice, a National Assembly – was also Ebert's programme. He simply felt better able and politically better placed than the Prince to implement it. Prince Max, who called on him in the afternoon to say goodbye, found him 'still endeavouring not to lose the organic continuity with the past'.

At noon when he took up the post of Reich Chancellor Ebert had been fairly confident that he would succeed in this. He found a well-run-in Government ready at hand and took it over – at first without making any changes in the cast. In one of the proclamations he issued in the afternoon he had addressed the civil servants in an almost supplicating, apologetic tone: 'I know that many will find it difficult to work with the new men but I appeal to your love of our people.' In any case, civil servants are not strike-prone. He was firmly in control of the SPD leadership, he had known since morning that he had the backing of the Army in Berlin.

To calm the working masses he was ready to take some of the Independents with him into the Government. He knew the Independents and was not afraid of them. They had been faithful SPD comrades under his Chairmanship until well into the War, and if in the course of time they had then split off, very few of them were firebrands or radicals. In the Cabinet they would be under his eye and their participation in the Government would furnish a handy alibi. When at noon in the Chancellery, on his way to the Reichstag and to his potato soup, he abruptly offered them coalition, he did it according to ear-witnesses 'pretty bluntly' and 'condescendingly'. At noon he still thought he held all the trump cards.

But by afternoon everything had gone seriously wrong. Scheidemann's uncalled-for proclamation of the Republic had been the first mishap; a second and more serious one was Prince Max's refusal to become Reich Administrator and his hurried departure. Ebert then had to come to terms with the idea of a republic as best he could – simply because there was no one left prepared to embody the monarchy. This he could learn to bear. But then the Independents had made unexpected difficulties; at first they had been unable to come to a decision about his offer of a coalition, finally they had stipulated unacceptably radical conditions. By evening no coalition had yet taken shape and Ebert had to content himself with nominating a few additional SPD Secretaries of State. His call for the streets to be emptied had fallen on deaf ears. At least the mass demonstrations had passed without much bloodshed, and by tomorrow, a Sunday, Ebert hoped that the masses would be tired, would want to stay at home and sleep off their revolutionary ardour.

But now all these hopes were dashed. Now it was clear that the Revolution would continue tomorrow, and in a much more dangerous, much more organized and more purposeful manner than today. A counter-force had shown its face which was competing with him for the leadership and which, in sharp contrast to his own aims, far from calling off the Revolution intended to fan it further. How could he get the better of it?

He had no prepared positions to which he could retreat. Ebert represented the extreme Left of the Establishment, the last reserve of the old order – which for him meant 'order' pure and simple. Behind Ebert there was no one. Take him away and there was nothing left.

Did this mean open warfare? Forbidding the elections for the councils and the meeting in the Busch Circus and, if necessary, using firearms to shoot them down? Ebert shrank back from this idea. Certainly, he had the support of the Army in Berlin. But could he expect them to go to any lengths? Were they in fact still a genuine, blindly obedient military force? Only a few hours ago Wels had persuaded them *not* to fire. Could they now suddenly be persuaded to fire again? And even if one could persuade them – should one? A bloodbath among Social Democrat workers perpetrated by the first Social Democrat Chancellor on the first day of his Government? Impossible!

That left only one way out: Ebert would have to renounce his attempt to maintain 'organic continuity with the past' through his own person. He would have to stop being the last Reich Chancellor and become instead the first Chairman of this – what was it called? – this 'Council of People's Representatives'. He would have to collect a second stamp of office: first that of Prince Max which had been unconventional enough, now that of the meeting in the Busch Circus. Impossible? No. There were after all enough loyal Social Democrats among Berlin's workers; it was merely a question of mobilizing them quickly enough. Above all the alliance with the Independents had to be signed and sealed even at the expense of concessions; the workers and soldiers in the Circus would have to be confronted with the *fait accompli* of an all-Socialist government. Reconciliation, unity, 'no fratricidal war' – that would have to be the slogan now. Ebert knew his workers well enough to know that this slogan would carry weight, that it was irresistible.

As for the soldiers, they too were meant to vote and they were, thank goodness, anything but revolutionary; earlier today it had been anyone's guess whether or not they would shoot the Revolution to bits. They had not done so in the end and it was perhaps no longer to be expected of them. But *voting* down the Revolution –

that they could still do. Here Otto Wels could be used again. He had done so well in the morning, he had hit the right note with the soldiers, he would have to get back into the barracks and get to work on the soldiers to make sure they voted the right way the following day.

In the end, when all this had been achieved, Ebert, having accomplished a coalition of the two Socialist parties, would have to appear personally in the Busch Circus and have himself elected 'revolutionary leader'. He would willy-nilly have to howl with the wolves for an hour or two. It was the only way. What Reich Chancellor Prince Max had seen in Reich Chancellor Ebert, Reich Chancellor Ebert saw – in the People's Commissar Ebert. If he was still to prevent the Revolution, he would have to begin by appearing to lead it. There was no other way, but this way it might still work.

Ebert summoned his party comrades back from the ante-room. He had reached a decision and issued his instructions. That very night his crew went to work, headed by the indefatigable Otto Wels still swollen with success. The men of the Revolutionary Shop Stewards also worked throughout the night. It was as though the staffs of two opposing armies were in active preparation on the eve of a decisive battle.

November 9, 1918 ticked to its end. It had brought the downfall of the monarchy but not yet the victory of the Revolution. During the night of November 9–10 the fate of the Revolution was still in the balance. Only the next day could decide it.

7. November 10: The Revolution's Battle of the Marne

Professor Ernst Troeltsch – theologian, professor of history and since 1914 one of the glories of Berlin University – sat down that very month to describe how the citizens of Berlin spent November 10:

On Sunday morning after a night of anxiety this picture emerged from the newspapers: the Kaiser in Holland, the revolution victorious in most centres, the Federal princes in the process of abdicating. Not one man has died for Kaiser and Reich! The civil service in the service of the new Government! All obligations will continue to be met and no run on the banks!

Sunday November 10, was a truly beautiful autumn day. As usual great numbers of citizens went walking in the *Grunewald*: no display of elegance, ordinary middle-class folk, some of them had perhaps taken care to dress simply; all somewhat subdued, like people whose fate is being decided somewhere far away, but relieved and at ease because it had gone off so well. Trams and underground trains ran as usual, a sort of pledge that the immediate necessities of life were secure. On all faces one could read: salaries will go on being paid.'

The citizens on their Sunday afternoon strolls in the Grunewald who were already feeling relieved because everything had 'gone off so well', did not suspect that their fate was in fact as yet to be decided on this Sunday afternoon – and not 'somewhere far away' but in the East of their own city, at a turbulent mass meeting in the Busch Circus where that afternoon the first great battle of the revolution was fought and lost – the first and at the same time the decisive battle: the Revolution's Battle of the Marne.

Saturday, November 9, had seen the climax of the spontaneous, leaderless Revolution which had broken out in Kiel the previous Monday. Sunday, November 10, saw the beginnings of its defeat.

Paradoxically, what was to put the seal on its defeat looked from the outside like its final and greatest triumph.

On that Sunday morning everything was still undecided. The streets in the city centre, where yesterday a mass of people had surged, lay empty in the Sunday calm. The flagstaffs in Unter den Linden still carried red flags – but there was barely a handful of isolated strollers to rejoice or glower at them. The workers, who yesterday at this time had been starting their great revolutionary march, were today – Sunday! – almost all back in their factories to elect the workers' councillors whose task it would be that afternoon in the Busch Circus to institute the new Government, the Government of the victorious Revolution. It was a brilliant organizational success for the Revolutionary Shop Stewards who had formed this plan late on Saturday evening. The news had spread by word of mouth and the workers had turned up almost in full strength to register their votes.

But they did not vote the way the Shop Stewards wanted them to. The SPD, too, had not been idle that night. Thousands of leaflets had been hurriedly drafted, printed, distributed. The Party newspaper, *Vorwärts*, was passed from hand to hand in all the factories that morning, or men read it in groups and stood there, gravely nodding their heads. Its leading article was headlined: 'No Fratricidal War.' With what seemed a touch of genius this headline hit on the general mood.

The mood was no longer that of the previous morning – a point the Shop Stewards had overlooked. Yesterday it had been bitter, impatient, rebellious, grimly determined, full of dammed-up, explosive anger; in fact, a mood of revolution. Today it was relaxed, tolerant, conciliatory – a mood of victory, not flushed with success but infused with gratitude. Everyone felt vaguely grateful that victory had been so easy, that there had been no battle, no casualties, no bloodshed. Those who the day before had marched into the city ready to die now felt as if they had been returned to life. Richard Müller, one of the leaders of the Revolutionary Shop Stewards, reports that in some factories they elected as workers' councillors SPD officials who had yesterday been forcibly ejected for refusing to join in the great march. There was no turning this great emotional tide. Certainly, most of the candidates put forward by the Revolutionary Shop Stewards got through, but a large number of the newly elected workers' councillors – this much the Shop Stewards angrily admitted to themselves by mid-day – were supporters of Ebert.

The elections in the factories had been a semi-defeat. In the barracks, defeat was total. Here the Revolutionary Shop Stewards carried no weight, here no one knew them, here Otto Wels did the talking and he pulled no punches. There was no talk here of reconciliation, of brotherhood – it was a question of foiling a sinister plot aimed at taking the SPD by surprise and keeping it out of government. Had not the soldiers yesterday taken the people's part without considerations of party? Very well then, it was now their duty to defend the people's rights. The soldiers must place themselves at the disposal of the Ebert–Scheidemann Government, following the example set yesterday by the Naumburg Fusiliers!

A roar of applause! It was immediately decided to form an action committee of the Berlin units. In the courtyard of the *Vorwärts* building, there was, at mid-day, a mass meeting of soldiers – elected and unelected ones. Leaders and speakers were appointed, rations distributed, and in the afternoon, long before the time for the meeting, the soldiers, with Wels at their head, marched in closed ranks to the Busch Circus where they occupied the front rows near the arena. Hermann Müller, later to become SPD Chancellor, throws light on their mood:

A Spartacist who on his way to the Lindenstrasse had joined the column of the soldiers' councillors out of curiosity, discovered what was going on and threatened Wels with a revolver, yelling like a man possessed: 'You dog, you are going to spoil everything for us!' But he did not fire and so he was not lynched.

In this manner, in factories and barracks during the morning and early afternoon of November 10, the defeat of the Revolution and Ebert's victory were taking shape. Ebert himself as yet knew nothing of this. He still looked on the Busch Circus meeting as a lion trainer might regard his first entry into the lion's cage and

he felt he could face it only if he came armed with a coalition with
the Independents, with a Government of Socialist reunification.
While the factories and barracks were busy electioneering and
electing, Ebert at the Chancellery was chairing a meeting of the
Reich Government – still Prince Max's old semi-bourgeois
Government; and at the same time the Parliamentary Party of the
Independents was meeting in the Reichstag. Both meetings were
concerned with the reshaping of the Government.

The Government meeting had also to consider whether the
Armistice conditions should be accepted or rejected but this point
was hardly raised; their acceptance was a matter of course. The
conditions were tough ones. They made it impossible for Germany to continue fighting. But it had been clear since September
29 that Germany could no longer fight. The meeting had received
a telegram from the High Command suggesting that they should
try to negotiate for concessions, but if this failed, they should sign
nevertheless: 'REQUEST SPEEDY DECISION GOVERNMENT ON THESE
LINES, VON HINDENBURG.' The Government decided accordingly.
Erzberger, who spent the day in Compiègne nervously waiting,
reports that late in the evening he received an uncoded cable
authorizing him to sign, 'which greatly upset me as the open
cable jeopardized the result of the two-day negotiations'. He
nevertheless achieved some concessions. 'The cable was signed
"Reich Chancellor End". The interpreting officer asked if "End"
was the name of the new Chancellor and who this gentleman
might be; the French High Command and the Government in
Paris had not heard of him. I explained that "End" meant full-
stop.'

All this happened on the fringe, as it were; the acceptance of the
Armistice conditions was no longer a problem. That morning
Ebert was really concerned with the decision of the Independents
– and in his present position he was prepared to accept their
conditions for participating in the Government almost as completely as the Armistice conditions. He now *needed* the Independents in his Government, needed them as urgently as Germany
needed the end of the War – or at least he thought he did. With
a Government of Socialist reconciliation he felt in control of the

situation; without such a Government he did not know how to cope with the afternoon's revolutionary assembly.

At 1.30 p.m. news came of his deliverance: the Independents, after hours of wavering, had decided to nominate three 'People's Commissars' to Ebert's Cabinet. Their conditions were harsh; the day before Ebert would have rejected them: political power in the hands of the workers' and soldiers' councils; delay of the decision about a National Assembly; all 'People's Commissars' to have equal status. Well, one would see. All that mattered now was to have the Independents in the Government. Their list of candidates was something of a relief: Hugo Haase, their Chairman, a gentle, melancholy man who usually conceded, albeit plaintively; Wilhelm Dittmann, a nobody; and the third, Emil Barth, one of the leaders of the Revolutionary Shop Stewards – not a bad idea, perhaps, to have him in the Government as a hostage. Ebert accepted conditions and candidates – without objection and without discussion. Then he sat down to a hasty lunch and to draft his speech for the meeting. He felt firmly in the saddle again.

In these early hours of the afternoon, before the decisive battle of the Busch Circus, a third meeting was being held: the Revolutionary Shop Stewards were holding a hasty council of war to agree on their tactics in the light of the new situation. In contrast with Ebert and Haase they already knew the result of the morning elections; they had been there, and they knew their cause had done badly. Now they had to hit on some new idea, and in fact, once again, they succeeded. Richard Müller reported:

After the result of the voting it was clear that the right-wing Socialists together with the right-wing Independents . . . had a majority. A Government without the right-wing Socialists was out of the question. They had to be taken into account. It was also clear to everyone that the right-wing Socialists would try to break the power of the workers' and soldiers' councils in order to bring about a National Assembly and as a result a bourgeois-democratic Government. If they succeeded, the Revolution was lost.

So what was to be done? Someone – there is no way of telling who – had the saving inspiration. If the formation of an Ebert

Revolutionaries take up defensive positions on the roof of the Brandenburg Gate in Berlin. (Photo: Staatsbibliotek, Berlin)

Demonstration in front of the House of Representatives in Berlin. The placard reads: 'All Power to the Workers' and Soldiers' Councils'.
(Photo: Ullstein)

Government could not be prevented, one would simply have to elect a second body, under some name or other, which could develop into a sort of counter-government. After all, the Shop Stewards as organizers of the meeting provided its Executive and fixed the agenda; with clever management it should be possible, in addition to the 'Council of People's Commissars' to call into being a second council packed with their men. As Richard Müller noted:

It was decided to propose to the meeting the election of an action committee of the workers' and soldiers' councils. Its tasks were not to be discussed, it was to come about without any debate, by a kind of bluff.

Both sides had thus laid their booby-traps. At five o'clock in the afternoon, while an early November dusk settled on Berlin and the citizens returned to their poorly heated homes from their afternoon walks, the Revolution and the bourgeois-parliamentary republic went into the ring in Busch Circus, in a seething witch's cauldron of two or three thousand people. Both fought under false flags. Ebert assumed the guise of a revolutionary. The revolutionaries assumed the guise of parliamentarians. The decision about who won or lost was in the hands of a mass meeting such as Germany has never seen before or since: in the front rows some thousand men in field grey uniforms, a firmly disciplined block; above them, towards the cupola, a thousand or two workers, men and women, blurred in the half-light – a world of feverish, care-worn faces, whose wretchedness has been captured for all time in the drawings of Heinrich Zille. In the arena, at improvised wooden tables, sat the panel – and all the VIPs of the Socialist parties, from Ebert to Liebknecht.

In the chair was Emil Barth, one of the leaders of the Revolutionary Shop Stewards and also a proposed People's Commissar; a man of great energy, with a thirst for action and not a little vanity, who saw himself as the Napoleon of the Revolution and was over-fond of the sound of his own voice. That afternoon, this was to be his undoing and the undoing of his cause.

Ebert, the first to speak, announced the conciliation of the two Socialist parties and carried the meeting at once: it was what they wanted to hear. The rest of his speech – patriarchal, strict and measured in tone as always – was also well in tune with the mood of the meeting. He had a lot to say about law and order, but order, he claimed, was necessary 'for the complete victory of the Revolution'. Haase, the leader of the Independents, who followed him, appeared feeble by comparison. He could only support him, and perhaps he betrayed the fact that at heart he had been against the coalition. It had been Haase's lot before, on this day as well as long ago on August 4, 1914, to announce in public Party decisions taken against his advice. When it was Liebknecht's turn to speak, he tried to swim against the tide. He berated the SPD with a list of their wartime sins. But in this euphoric moment of victory and reconciliation, no one wanted to hear. There was much heckling; down below at the rim of the arena the soldiers became restless. They chanted in unison: 'Unity! Unity!'

Then it was time to count the votes, and the moment had come – quite casually and without any fuss, before anyone woke up to what was happening – to elect the action committee. The panel of the meeting, that is to say the Revolutionary Shop Stewards, had a list of committee members up their sleeves. But now Emil Barth made his big mistake. Instead of simply calling for votes, and quite against the agenda, he made a fourth long speech – perhaps to counteract Liebknecht's, or simply because he enjoyed the sound of his own voice. Richard Müller, who was suffering agonies in the seat next to him, noted: 'The attentive listener could grasp the hidden intentions between Barth's lines.' Ebert, in particular, grasped them. He asked to speak again and declared briefly and firmly that such a committee was 'superfluous', but if it had to be formed, then like the Government it would have to be filled by both parties in parity. From the list he had just heard, the SPD was absent. Whereupon Barth finally gave the game away. In this committee, he shouted excitedly, there was no room for right-wing Socialists. With that the fat was in the fire. Richard Müller writes:

What followed on Barth's declaration can hardly be described. The soldiers shouted in wild confusion 'Unity, parity! Parity!' Captain von Beerfelde submitted a list from the soldiers. The right-wing Socialist

Büchel [whom, according to the other Müller, Hermann Müller, Barth had tried to prevent from speaking by poking him in the back with the presidential bell] came up with a list from his Party. Richard Müller and Karl Liebknecht attempted to speak against parity on the committee; they were both shouted down. The excitement escalated into frenzy. The soldiers rushed into the arena and on to the rostrum. They threatened to carry on with the Revolution without the workers, without the parties, and to install a military government. There was such a tumult that for some time it was impossible to carry on with the meeting.

With the meeting interrupted, the soldiers going wild in the lower rows and the workers in the upper rows engaged in bewildered discussions with each other, there was feverish negotiation in the arena – under the eyes of the agitated crowd, but not within their hearing, for microphones were not yet invented. Both sides were suddenly anxious, and made rash and ill-considered proposals. For a brief moment the SPD offered to content itself with two members out of a total of eleven, for a brief moment the Shop Stewards were ready to forgo the whole action committee. But this was suddenly opposed by the SPD itself: what an impression that would make! Alright, an evenly manned committee then, but they would have to agree here and now on its composition. Someone proposed Liebknecht, but Liebknecht flatly refused. Never would he sit at the same table as Ebert's men! When agreement seemed finally within reach, the soldiers raised new difficulties; now they demanded a double parity, not only as between SPD and USPD, but also as between workers and soldiers. It was getting late, a decision would have to be reached, they would agree to this too. But now the soldiers could not agree on their own representatives. Finally the meeting was declared open again, and as peace gradually returned, Barth announced the formation of a twenty-man 'executive council of the workers' and soldiers' councils': ten soldiers, ten workers, half of the latter to be composed of members of the SPD, half of nominees proposed by the Shop Stewards. The soldiers' representatives would be chosen tomorrow. The meeting accepted the proposal: it was by now ready to accept almost anything. It was fairly late. It was past supper-time, many were hungry (people were hungry in Germany in those days) and many had a long way to go home. Everything suddenly happened very quickly. They confirmed the new Reich Government which was to call itself 'the Council of People's Commissars', and they carried a previously prepared resolution with a lot of ornate and beautiful words about the Socialist Republic and World Revolution (the bourgeois papers printed it the next day, not so *Vorwärts*). Then they sang the 'International' and at last – night had fallen – the Busch Circus began to empty.

None of the main protagonists went home satisfied. The *Obleute* knew they had lost their battle. Ebert now had revolutionary endorsement for his counter-revolutionary Government and little to fear from the executive committee in its new shape. But Ebert, too, was depressed: he had won, indeed; he had kept the reins in his hands, but at what cost! The Independents in the Government, this suspicious executive committee as a parallel government, he himself no longer Reich Chancellor but the 'People's Commissar', revolutionary leader against his will, annexed, as it were, by the Revolution he had wanted to bring to a halt and call off. Would he go on enjoying the confidence of his bourgeois colleagues in Parliament and Cabinet and of the High Command in Spa? He felt himself pushed into a false position. He had always hated the Revolution; now he hated it doubly for forcing him, an honest man, to turn liar and traitor. For he had no doubt about one thing: if he still wanted to undo the Revolution – and he could not help but want this – he would have to betray it. He was condemned to play a double game. Could he still bring it off? Would the state and the society he wanted to serve still be prepared, after today, to accept him as their saviour?

On this score, at least, he was reassured late that evening by an unexpected telephone call. It came through on a secret line, the existence of which Ebert had until then been unaware. Spa was at the other end, the High Command, General Groener. At last a decent person with whom one could talk sensibly! The exact nature of this almost legendary telephone call has never been made known; there were no tape recorders in those days, and there were no witnesses. But subsequent statements by Groener give an approximate indication of what must have been said (Ebert never talked about it). The General offered loyal co-operation – and made demands: a fight against radicalism and Bolshevism, an end as soon as possible to the 'councils nonsense', a National Assembly, a return to 'a state of order'. Ebert was able to agree to all this with real feeling; it was exactly what he himself wanted. He must have opened his heart to Groener; for Groener later noted that, to judge from the conversation, Ebert 'was clinging to the helm with difficulty and near to being overrun by the Independents and the Liebknecht lot'. Evidently he was still in the grip of the turbulent meeting he had just been through. At the end, Ebert thanked the General – not the reverse.

Groener later spoke of a 'pact' which he had concluded that evening with Ebert. It was a pact to fight against the Revolution whose leadership Ebert had accepted not many hours earlier. 'Ebert agreed to my suggestion of a pact,' Groener writes. 'From then on we consulted with each other every evening about the necessary measures, using a secret line between the Chancellery and the High Command. The pact proved itself.'

8. *Between Revolution and Counter-Revolution*

Theodor Wolff, at that time one of the best known of German journalists, wrote in the *Berliner Tageblatt* of November 10:

Like a suddenly unleashed storm the greatest of all revolutions has overthrown the imperial regime, with all that was part of it, from top to bottom. One may call it the greatest of all revolutions because never has a *Bastille* so firmly built and so solidly walled about been taken at the first assault. A week ago there was still a structure of military and civil administration so extensively ramified, inter-twined and deeply rooted that its reign seemed safe from the changing times. The grey motor-cars of the officers raced through the streets of Berlin, policemen stood in the public squares like pillars, a gigantic military organization seemed to embrace everything, in public offices and ministries an apparently invincible bureaucracy was enthroned. Yesterday morning all this was still there, at least in Berlin. Yesterday afternoon nothing remained.

He was wrong – perhaps it looked like that on November 10, but the truth was different. In fact the state had barely been scratched. On the Monday after Revolution Weekend the same civil servants went back to the same public offices, and even the policemen (who on Saturday afternoon had been glad to get home unmolested) were back again a few days later; in the armies in the field in the East and West the same generals and officers remained in command, and even the Reich Government was in effect unchanged – except that at its head, instead of an Imperial Reich Chancellor, there was now a six-man collegium of 'People's Commissars' among whom one, in effect, was still Reich Chancellor: Ebert. All the staunchly conservative country prefects, provincial prime ministers, ministry officials were at their desks as ever. Not one of them had been removed; they had merely had a few workers' councillors planted over their heads and treated this as extreme provocation. Their mood – and that of large sections of the bourgeoisie – was expressed by another journalist, Paul Baecker. He wrote, also on November 10, in the conservative *Deutsche Tageszeitung*:

Words cannot suffice to express the indignation and the grief . . . the great edifice for which our fathers fought with their blood – wiped out by treason in the ranks of our own people! Germany, yesterday still unconquered, now left at the mercy of her enemies by men bearing the name of Germans, forced to her knees in ignominious disgrace by felony in her own ranks!

The German socialists knew that peace was in the offing, that it was merely a matter of facing the enemy for a few weeks, perhaps only a few days, with a firm unbreached front, to extract tolerable conditions from him. In this situation they hoisted the white flag.

This is a perfidy that can never and shall never be forgiven. It is an act of treason, not only towards the Monarchy and the Army, but towards the German people who will have to bear the consequences through centuries of decline and of misery.

Baecker's attack was as inaccurate as Wolff's hymn to 'the greatest of all revolutions'. It was not the Socialists who had waved the white flag, but Ludendorff; delay could not improve, but merely worsen the Armistice conditions, and there was no question of treason. Nor were centuries of misery and decline in prospect. But Baecker no doubt honestly felt what he wrote – and expressed the feelings of millions: of the officers whose insignia of rank had been torn off, of the conservative officials suddenly having to wrangle with workers' councillors, of the whole bourgeoisie watching its world collapse, and also of simpler people with rigidly 'national' views, for example Lance-Corporal Hitler who threw himself sobbing on to his hospital bed in Pasewalk and, weeping tears of rage, swore to become a politician. At the same time as the Revolution, the counter-Revolution was born, and here, as early as November 10, its authentic voice was to be heard. It is worth noting that this article could be printed in Berlin on November 10, 1918 without hindrance. Never has a revolution from the very first moment allowed its enemies such unlimited freedom to agitate and protest as did the German Revolution of 1918.

Not that its enemies offered any thanks for this. The then Mrs Ludendorff (his first wife Margaret, not his second, later famous, wife, Mathilde) says of her husband:

After the Revolution Ludendorff repeatedly declared: 'The revolutionaries' greatest piece of stupidity was to leave us all alive. Well, if I ever come to power again, there will be no pardons. With a good conscience I would have Ebert, Scheidemann and company strung up and dangling!'

Ebert, Scheidemann and company – not, that is to say, simply Liebknecht and Rosa Luxemburg who at least really wanted the Revolution. Ebert and Scheidemann did not want it at all; on the contrary, they had striven to the last moment to prevent it, and from the first moment of their victory were solely occupied with stopping it, rolling it back and if possible undoing it. But for Ludendorff – and for the many embittered members and supporters of the old ruling class who reacted in the same way – they were revolutionaries, traitors and 'November criminals'; and in fact the Revolution had raised them to the pinnacle of power – they were now 'People's Commissars'; whether they liked it or not, they from now on embodied the Revolution – in the eyes of the counter-revolutionaries as much as in those of the revolutionaries. From the first moment of their government they found themselves caught between revolution and counter-revolution.

It was their tragedy – or tragi-comedy – that they could not see this. They could not, or would not, see that since November 9 they had made millions of enemies – enemies to the death – on the Right; they could only see their old familiar enemies on the Left. Scheidemann, for instance, as late as December 29 during a critical Cabinet meeting: 'Of course there are a dozen officers capable of crazy pranks. But it is on the other side that those stand who endanger the Revolution. Against them we must defend ourselves.' And the third SPD 'People's Commissar', a Dr Otto Landsberg, said on the same occasion: 'There is always so much talk of a threatening counter-Revolution . . . The essential difference between this Revolution and all earlier ones is that all power structures of the overthrown class have been so completely shaken and eliminated that the danger of counter-revolution can only become acute if the people on the extreme Left succeed in driving the masses to despair.' Finally, Herman Müller, later an SPD Reich Chancellor: 'I must tell you openly, since November 9 I have not been afraid of counter-revolution for a single day.'

In fact Ebert and his political friends were at heart still living in October – in the time when the *Kaiserreich*, tottering and about to fall, had taken these 'unpatriotic outcasts' courteously to its bosom, passed them the buck of defeat and made them welcome as helpers in need. They had done their honest best to help it in its need; they had not been able to save the Monarchy; they were still trying to save everything else. For them the Revolution was a misunderstanding or a regrettable incident which they still hoped to reverse.

But it was irreversible – even after it had been choked off and crushed. What had happened in Germany, quite against the wishes of the Social Democrat leadership, between November 4 and 9, had torn aside the artificial fog of October and left clear-cut political fronts. The insincere pretence of peace between High Command and the Reichstag majority, between militarism and parliamentarism, Ludendorff's finely spun plan to present the Social Democrats and their bourgeois allies with the illusion of power in order to burden them with the responsibility for the defeat while the military stayed in the background and wielded the real power – all this had been swept aside in the week of revolution by the spontaneous action of the Social Democrat masses of the workers and soldiers.

The revolution of the masses gave the Social Democrat leaders their first and only chance to grasp real power – at the expense of the poisoned power borrowed from Ludendorff on September 29. Once the officers had had their insignia torn off and the 'general commands' had been replaced by workers' and soldiers' councils, there was no possibility of reconciliation, not even for appearances' sake. The question of who would rule had been asked – and on November 9 it seemed for a moment as if it had been answered. The military dictatorship which had ruled Germany to that day, had gone under almost without resistance.

4*

If the Social Democrat leadership now made use of the victory of its supporters, renounced the October agreement with the High Command, completed the defeat of the old military authorities and created its own revolutionary forces, it would no longer have to fear the revenge of powerless generals and officers. But if it permitted them to rise again and to recover from the degrading and stunning blow they had sustained in November, then it could expect no mercy – no mercy not only for its own revolutionary supporters who had dared to 'mutiny', but also for itself. By allowing themselves to be turned by the Revolution into 'People's Commissars', Ebert, Scheidemann and Landsberg had, in the eyes of the offended officers, identified themselves with the Revolution.

They continued to play a double game, not noticing that they were playing it to their own disadvantage. They still called themselves revolutionaries – and their words were noted and later used in evidence against them. In their actions they remained counter-revolutionaries – without earning the gratitude of the real counter-Revolution. But the masses who had given them their confidence on November 9 and 10 gradually noticed what was going on and turned against them. In two months the ambivalent game played by Ebert and the SPD was to lead to civil war.

*

What was at issue during these two months? If one were to listen to the SPD politicians of the time and their later historians, the issue was one of dictatorship by the councils versus parliamentary democracy, of keeping Bolshevism at bay and of electing a National Constituent Assembly. But this was propaganda – and still is today. The truth had a different face. In truth the only issue was between Revolution and counter-Revolution.

Germany in 1918 was at no point threatened by a Bolshevik dictatorship; for the simple reason that the essential instrument of power, a Bolshevik party capable of dictating, did not exist. Karl Liebknecht and Rosa Luxemburg had no organization whatever until December 30, 1918, and only a very feeble one thereafter; nothing to compare with Lenin's corps of professional revolutionaries prepared by fourteen years of training. They were powerless individuals who were limited to agitating and to what the Berlin *Obleute* contemptuously called 'revolutionary gymnastics': repeated aimless demonstrations by which the participants hoped to get themselves into a revolutionary fervour. In Germany in the autumn of 1918 the 'Bolshevik danger' was a bogey, not a reality.

On the other hand the elections to a National Assembly were not a major point of disagreement. The only point being contested was their timing – which was, of course, not without importance. The Independents were anxious to postpone them as long as possible, into the spring of 1919, to give the Revolution time to consolidate. The SPD wanted the elections to be held as soon as possible, to give the National Assembly a chance to carry on where the old Reichstag had left off, as if no revolution had taken place. But by the end of November a compromise had been reached: February 16 as the day for the elections. In the middle of December it was paradoxically the highest organ of the Revolution, the National Congress of Councils itself, which put the date forward to January 19 – conclusive proof that the Councils did not want their own dictatorship and that the confrontation – Council dictatorship versus parliamentary democracy – simply did not exist.

In fact something quite different was at stake. The Councils – the installing of workers' and soldiers' councils had been the main manifestation of the Revolution, and the counter-Revolution's first aim was to abolish them – had no objection to parliamentary democracy. They did not regard themselves as a substitute for a parliament, but as an instrument for the radical reform and democratization of the *executive*, that is to say the essential body of the state, the administration and in particular the military structure. It was the old conservative bureaucracy and the old conservative corps of officers which the Councils were striving to get under control, eradicate and reshape from the roots upwards. The workers and soldiers who had carried through the Revolution knew instinctively that as long as the old bureaucracy and the old corps of officers retained their power, the Revolution was lost; the most magnificent constitution and the most magnificent parliament would be of no avail. Real power had its seat in the administration, in police headquarters and the 'general commands', and also in the courts; if the old entrenched powers were left untouched, they would grasp the first opportunity to take their revenge on the Revolution. There was no room for compromise. On this field the victory of Revolution or counter-Revolution would be decided.

And on this field Ebert and the SPD leadership took up positions clearly on the side of the counter-Revolution. They were anxious to save what the Revolution was anxious to overthrow: the old state and form of society, embodied in the bureaucracy and officers' corps. They wanted to parliamentarize the old state and form part of it, joining in its future government. But the thought of the disorder which would inevitably follow any attempt really to revolutionize it, filled them with horror. *That is why* they wanted to be rid of the Councils as quickly as possible; *that is why* – quite against the wish of the majority of the Councils – they misrepresented them as an alternative to a National Assembly; and *that is why* they readily incorporated into their propaganda the bourgeois misconception that government by the Councils was the same thing as Bolshevism.

In fact there were hardly any Spartacists in the Councils – Liebknecht applied in vain for a seat in the Reich Congress of Councils – the SPD from the beginning had the majority in almost all local Councils, and this picture was more than confirmed when provincial and regional Councils were elected at the beginning of December. One could go as far as to say that the Councils were the living body of the SPD, its active members and officials (a minority was drawn from members of the USPD and there were also a few bourgeois members, particularly in the Soldiers' Councils); they regarded themselves as loyal auxiliaries of the Government.

This is where the tragic misunderstanding lay. For Ebert's Government was no revolutionary government; it saw itself, in Ebert's subsequent words, simply as the receiver and liquidator of the *Kaiserreich*. It was the loyal servant of those who since November 9 had become its bitter enemies, and fought without mercy against those who felt themselves to be its shield-bearers. On their side the Councils, too, stood firm against their best friends: they wanted no truck with the Spartacists who were demanding the dictatorship of the Councils; they merely wanted to equip the Social Democrat state with a Social Democrat executive. No one saw this more clearly than Liebknecht and Rosa Luxemburg. Liebknecht, for instance, wrote on November 20:

Often the elected workers have very little enlightenment, very little class-consciousness, so that the workers' councils . . . have no revolutionary character at all.

And Rosa Luxemburg, ten days later, wrote:

If the Revolution were going on in those of its organs which were the creation of its early days, the Workers' and Soldiers' Councils, it would be in dire straits . . . The Revolution will live without the Councils, the Councils without the Revolution are dead.

Even the Social Democrat leaders could hardly fail to notice that the Councils were not staffed with Spartacists, but with their own people. Nevertheless the Councils were a thorn in their flesh from the start. They had not been anticipated, did not fit into their programme, they prevented an alliance with the bourgeois parties and with the High Command. They had to go. From the start Ebert and Scheidemann treated the Councils not only with distrust and hostility, but with spite and malice. Scheidemann, addressing the Reich Congress of Councils, said:

I am of the firm persuasion that the permanent institution of workers' and soldiers' Councils would mean – I say this after due consideration – the absolutely certain downfall of the Reich.

Of course it was easy to find fault with the Councils. They lacked the administrative experience of the old civil servants, the military skill of the staff officers. Where could they have acquired them? Their intervention brought disorder in its wake – has there ever been a revolution without disorder? Nevertheless, most of the spiteful attacks on the 'chaos' of the 'council hotchpotch' (*Rätewirtschaft*) spread by the counter-Revolution and eagerly picked up by the SPD leaders, were vastly exaggerated. The Councils did not consist of corrupt, pleasure-seeking revolutionary bohemians; they were largely composed of sober and solid, thoughtful working men, party and trade union officials, as fond of order in their own way as the old civil servants they were seeking to control and replace. In the course of four weeks they had largely overcome the original chaos and created an organization parallel with the old administrative bodies and fully capable of functioning at all levels – an achievement commanding respect. Eberhard Kolb, who wrote the standard work *The Workers' Councils in German Home Politics 1918/19* (*Die Arbeiterräte in der Deutschen Innenpolitik 1918/19*), says that at the beginning of December the council organization 'provided the new Government and Party leadership with a politically reliable instrument in the reconstruction of the state which was there for them to use if they so chose'.

But they chose to do the opposite. They wanted to 'create order' – which meant re-establishing the old order – with the very instrument the Kaiser had wanted to use for this purpose on November 8: with the Army in the field, released by the Armistice and marching home from the West. That was the meaning of the 'pact' between Ebert and General Groener.

Later, in the course of the so-called 'stab-in-the-back' hearings in Munich in 1925, Groener was explicit on this subject. Here is his statement:

At first it was a question of wrenching power from the workers' and soldiers' Councils in Berlin. An operation was planned for this purpose, the military entry of ten divisions into Berlin. The People's Commissar Ebert was completely in agreement with this. An officer was despatched to Berlin to negotiate the details, also with the Prussian War Minister [still, as before November 9, von Scheüch] who had of course to be consulted. There were a number of difficulties. I may just mention that some Independent members of the Government, but also, I think, some soldiers' councillors – I cannot off-the-cuff be sure of the details – demanded that the troops move in without live ammunition. We naturally opposed this at once, and Herr Ebert naturally agreed that the troops should move into Berlin with live ammunition. For this entry by the troops which was to afford us at the same time an opportunity to re-establish a firm government in Berlin – I am now giving evidence under oath, the gentleman has asked me, therefore I must in God's name speak out about something which for good reasons I have not done before – a day-by-day military plan had been elaborated. This plan set out what was to happen: the disarming of Berlin, clearing Berlin of Spartacists, etc. All this had been provided for, day by day, for the individual divisions.'

The 'plan', worked out with General Staff precision, was made public much later, in 1940. It contains such points as:

Whoever is found in possession of arms without a licence is to be shot. Whoever keeps war material, including motor vehicles, will be summarily convicted. Deserters and sailors have to report to the nearest reserve unit or regional command within ten days. Whoever assumes an official function without authorization is to be shot. Unsafe parts of the city to be combed. Decrees about the unemployed and about emergency public works. The authority of officers to be restored in full (insignia, duty to salute, decorations, wearing of arms, badges for the army in the field). The administration and the troops to resume their legal functions. All substitute units to be disbanded at once.

Groener's statement in the witness box went on:

The officer I had sent to Berlin discussed all this with Herr Ebert. I am especially grateful to Herr Ebert for this and have defended him against all attacks for his absolute love of the Fatherland and his complete dedication to the cause. This plan had been formed throughout with Herr Ebert's knowledge and agreement.

The Ebert–Groener plan was to be put into effect from December 10 to 15. The first National Congress of Councils was planned for December 16, in Berlin. Evidently the 're-establishment of order' by ten divisions of the army returning from the front was intended to forestall it.

But nothing came of it. The counter-Revolution did not take place on this occasion, and the Congress of Councils met as arranged, little suspecting what fate it had narrowly escaped.

At first a few units of the Berlin garrison – having played a double-edged part from the outset of the Revolution and evidently having got wind of what was in the offing – acted prematurely. On Friday, December 6, something happened which Scheidemann was later to describe as a 'crazy prank', Richard Müller as a 'farce'. A unit of the *Franzer* regiment occupied the Prussian House of Representatives and arrested the executive council of the Berlin workers' and soldiers' Councils which moved there after its election in the Busch Circus on November 10 and had endeavoured to fulfil its functions with varying success. A detachment of Guard Fusiliers stopped a Spartacist demonstration march at the corner of Invalidenstrasse and Chausseestrasse and without warning fired into it with machine-guns. There were sixteen dead and many wounded. Another detachment of the *Franzer* regiment appeared outside the Reich Chancellery, called upon Ebert to come out – which he did more readily than usual – and proclaimed him Reich President. A Sergeant Spiro made a speech. He ended his oration with: 'So let us give a cheer for the German Republic and the great Fritz Ebert, whom, speaking from your midst, backed by armed power and conscious of speaking for the whole nation, I proclaim President of Germany.'

Ebert neither agreed nor refused. He would first have to talk to his friends in the Government. Then the matter was dropped – until, two months later, on February 11, 1919, the Weimar National Assembly made him Reich President after all. This time it had evidently been premature: the whole exercise went up in smoke. Whether Ebert knew of it in advance has never been clarified. In any case no one was ever taken to task for what was in effect an attempted *coup d'état*. The soldiers went back to their barracks, the men behind it remained unidentified, the executive council was restored to freedom. It was as if nothing had happened. Only the dead of the Chausseestrasse remained dead.

Four days later, on December 10, the returning field divisions marched into Berlin according to plan – not exactly in parade order but in good marching order and with live ammunition. Ebert – who had never shown himself to the masses of the workers on November 9 – welcomed them at the Brandenburg Gate with an extravagant speech: 'No enemy has vanquished you! Now Germany's unity is in your hands!'

But again nothing came of it. The plan to re-establish order and a 'firm' government in Berlin was not put into action and for years no one discovered that it had ever been contrived.

What happened was simply this: immediately after Ebert's speech of welcome the troops began to disperse – spontaneously, in breach of discipline, beyond recall. Neither Groener nor Ebert had taken the men's state of mind into account: the War was over, they were all glad to have survived it, they all wanted to get home – and Christmas was round the corner. There was no holding them. When they took up their quarters on the evening of the day of their arrival, they were already below strength, the next day their numbers had dwindled further, and two weeks later, out of ten divisions only some eight hundred men remained. In the words of Groener: 'The troops developed such an urge to get home that these ten divisions were absolutely of no use and the whole plan of clearing Berlin of Bolshevist elements, the surrendering of arms, etc., could simply not be put into effect.' For the time being the counter-Revolution had drawn a blank.

Instead, on December 16, the National Congress of Councils assembled in the Prussian House of Representatives at the Leipziger Platz in Berlin, as arranged. This was no longer a turbulent mass gathering like the revolutionary meeting of Berlin workers' and soldiers' councillors in the Busch Circus on November 10. A very orderly assembly, much like a parliament, now came together in Berlin, reminding journalist eye-witnesses irresistibly of pre-war SPD party congresses: the same types, often the same faces even, the same atmosphere, conducted under the same direction, with the same concern for order and respectability. What in the old days had been the Party's left-wing minority was now the Independents, that was the only difference. The majority loyally supported the party executive.

This majority in the Congress of Councils, in keeping with Ebert's wishes, decided to bring forward the date of the elections for a National Assembly; it expressly rejected a proposal by the Independents that the Congress itself should in the meantime assume ultimate legislative as well as executive power; having instituted a 16-man Central Council to replace the former Berlin executive council formed on November 10, it did not even empower it to pass interim legislation until the National Assembly could meet. The Independents thereupon decided grimly to boycott this Central Council which thus became a purely SPD organ. In this manner the first National Congress of Councils demonstrated its good faith and its good nature.

And yet this tame and well-disposed Congress of Councils brought about the great split between Party leadership and Party membership, the crisis of the Revolution and the civil war which exploded in January 1919. For on one point it remained inexorable: there was to be no comeback for the military dictatorship overthrown by the Revolution, the power of the generals and the officers' corps was to remain broken for good. On a proposal by the Hamburg delegation the Congress adopted by a big majority a resolution for the complete reorganization of the military structure, which became known as the 'Hamburg points': supreme command to rest with the People's Commissars under the control of the Central Council; disciplinary powers to be wielded by the soldiers' councils; free election of officers; no insignia of rank; no deference to superior officers outside service hours.

The essentially anti-militarist nature of the Revolution was once again made manifest. Its aims in all other directions may have been moderate or undecided, on this point it meant business. Most of the delegates already knew from their own experience that it was precisely the officers' corps which harboured the threat of counter-revolution. Many brought bad news about what happened in West German cities when the troops came marching back – arrest and maltreatment of workers' councillors, burning of red flags, secret orders about the forming of volunteer battalions in case of civil war. No one as yet suspected Ebert. No one knew of his pact with Groener.

The adoption of the 'Hamburg points' struck at the heart of this pact and set the crisis in motion. Hindenburg wired at once that he 'did not recognize' the Congress of Councils' resolution. Groener travelled to Berlin and threatened to resign if the 'Hamburg points' were implemented. The three People's Commissars of the USPD also threatened to resign – if the 'Hamburg points' were *not* implemented. Ebert strove to gain time: the detailed implementation had yet to be decided, he pointed out by way of consolation. (Groener: 'Ebert like few others was a master of the art of evasion.')

The High Command meanwhile began to muster volunteer battalions on the parade grounds around Berlin – tough, reliable, well-equipped instruments of counter-revolution which would not disperse like the ten returning divisions. And the troops in Berlin, who had so far opted for the Revolution, even if in a somewhat ambiguous manner, began to get restless.

While the inhabitants of Berlin were getting ready for their first paltry peacetime Christmas – there were no Christmas geese and no Christmas cakes, no Christmas tree candles; instead, black-market cartridge cases filled with carbide which could be tied to the branches and lit to give a stinking glow – the political atmosphere of Berlin turned as threateningly sultry as it had been before the weekend of the revolution. And then, on Christmas Eve, the storm broke. On December 24, 1918, Berlin was awakened by the roar of cannons.

9. *The Christmas Crisis*

In the morning hours of December 24, 1918 Revolution and Counter-Revolution fought a bloody battle on the Schlossplatz in Berlin. Revolution won. Then it gave victory away. You might say it handed it to the Counter-Revolution by way of a Christmas present.

In every revolution the attitude of armed power is the decisive factor. The final weeks of 1918 appear in such an uncertain light, not only because the Social Democrats' 'People's Commissars' played a double game, but chiefly because from week to week, even from day to day, no one could say for certain where the armed power stood, or even what it was composed of. The Armistice had been followed by disorganized, uncontrollable demobilization. The troops from the front, whom Ebert and Groener had hoped to use in the middle of December to liquidate the Revolution, were not alone in dispersing as soon as they got home; there was no holding the troops at home who had made the Revolution in early November; they, too, wanted to spend Christmas with their families. Only the officers were left – and those among the men who liked being soldiers; the Revolution had been made by those who disliked it. The Berlin garrison which still held the balance of power had shown as early as December 6 that in its present composition it was of more use to the Counter-Revolution than to the Revolution. To put it at its lowest, it had become an unknown quantity, under the influence of Otto Wels who had worked on the soldiers so successfully on November 9 and 10 and had since been appointed City Commander.

But there was an exception: the People's Naval Division, which had not been in existence on November 9 but had since come to be regarded as the Guards of the Revolution. Its nucleus was formed of several hundred sailors who had reached Berlin from

Kiel during the week of the Revolution, had at first been arrested there but had been freed on November 9. They were joined by a further several hundred sailors who were at home in Berlin; and finally by two thousand expressly summoned from Kiel by Wels on November 12. At times comprising three thousand men, the People's Naval Division was, during November, regarded as the Revolution's élite unit. On November 15, on orders from the City Commander, they had taken over the palace which had earlier been looted. Their staff was now billeted there, with the troops in the *Marstall*, the royal stables, opposite.

For four weeks the People's Naval Division was the pride of the Berlin city command. Then there was a sudden change. Whether because the division had refused to take part in the uprising of December 6 and had deposed its commanding officer for being involved in it, or because it was an obvious obstacle in the way of the Groener plan for the 're-establishment of order in Berlin', or simply because the wind had changed and they no longer fitted into the picture; from the middle of December onwards City Commander Wels, either on his own initiative or acting on hints from higher up, worked unmistakably towards their disbandment.

If you want to drown your dog, accuse it of rabies, says a French proverb. The People's Naval Division was suddenly suspected of being 'Spartacist' and was now held to blame for the looting of the palace, which they had, in fact, put a stop to. They were to be moved from the palace and their strength reduced to six hundred men. (Demobilization had already reduced numbers to about one thousand.) To bring pressure to bear, Wels held back their pay. And Christmas was approaching.

It sounds grotesque: because a unit of a thousand men felt cheated out of their Christmas pay – that is why a bloody street battle was waged in Berlin, that is why the Government split, that is what led to the final line-up in the civil war, that is how the Revolution got and lost its last chance. It sounds like an operetta. But the ridiculous thinly veils the grimly serious. It was not in fact merely the Christmas pay of the People's Naval Division which was at stake, it was its very existence, and as things now were,

Nr. 292. 35. Jahrg.

10 Pfennig

Vorwärts

Berliner Volksblatt.

Zentralorgan der sozialdemokratischen Partei Deutschlands.

Redaktion: SW. 68, Lindenstraße 3. · Fernsprecher: Amt Moritzplatz. Nr. 15190–15197. · Mittwoch, den 23. Oktober 1918. · Expedition: SW. 68, Lindenstraße 3. · Herausgeber: Karl Wengels, Nr. 15190–151977

Die Reichstagssitzung vom 22. Oktober.

Liebknecht aus dem Zuchthaus entlassen.

Nr. 40 — Jahrgang 1918 · Mittwoch, 25. Dezember 1918 · Preis 10 Pfs.

Die Rote Fahne

Zentralorgan des Spartakusbundes

Redaktion: Berlin SW 68, Wilhelmstr. 114 II. Fernspr.: Amt Kurfürst 8754 u. 2385. Expedition: Berlin SW 68, Friedrichstr. Prinz 1776. Fernspr.: Amt Zitzow 5735. Buch-Auslieferung: Möckernstr. 144, Erdgeschoß (am Anhalter Bahnhof). | Schriftleitung: **Karl Liebknecht und Rosa Luxemburg** | Abonnementspreis für Inland monatlich 1.50 M. Ausland monatlich 3.00 M. Anzeigenpreis: die Zarbollener Nonparelle-Zeile 75 Pf. Kleine Anzeigen: Überschriftswort 30 Pf., jedes weitere Wort 15 Pf.

Eberts Blutweihnacht.

Matrosen haben nicht kapituliert. — Halten Schloß und Marstall besetzt. — Sicherheitsmannschaften und Teil der Soldatenwehr kämpfen auf Seite der Matrosen. — Teil Ebert'scher Truppen fraternisiert. — Feindliche Truppen meist entwaffnet. — Ultimatum von 10 Minuten. — Artillerie

Morgen-Ausgabe

Berliner Tageblatt und Handels-Zeitung erscheint wöchentlich zwölfmal. Bezugspreis ...

Berliner Tageblatt

Nr. 576 · 47. Jahrgang · und Handels-Zeitung · Sonntag 10. November 1918

Der Erfolg der Revolution.

Headlines from three contemporary newspapers, October–December, 1918.

practically the very existence of the Revolution. The story of Christmas 1918 indeed made history: a chapter in German history at which one never knows whether to laugh or cry.

Throughout the week before Christmas the sailors' spokesmen were negotiating with Wels at the City Command. They were demanding their pay. Wels was demanding that they should first evacuate the palace. The sailors asked that Wels should first allocate them new staff quarters. It is not clear whether this was finally agreed. At any rate, nothing happened: the sailors did not get new staff quarters, they did not evacuate the palace and they did not get paid. And now Christmas was imminent.

On December 23, the sailors' patience ran out. At noon their leaders and spokesmen went, not to the command, but to the Reich Chancellery. There they encountered a state of crisis. The 'Coalition of Socialist Unity', formed on November 10, was on the point of breaking apart. Between the three SPD and the three USPD People's Commissars there was mistrust, irritability and open disagreement. The sailors could not but notice that the Independents treated them as friends, the SPD people as enemies. At last they were sent packing with this verdict: Hand over the keys of the palace, then you will get your pay. There was no mention of other staff quarters. The sailors were not told where they should hand in the keys.

At 4 p.m. the sailors were back in the Reich Chancellery, with the keys, but also with an armed escort who stationed themselves at the entrance. The sailors, headed by their leader, a Lieutenant Dorrenbach, asked to be taken to Emil Barth, one of the three USPD People's Commissars, and handed him the keys. Barth reached for the telephone and told Wels that he had the keys and Wels should now pay up. Wels refused on the grounds that he took instructions only from Ebert. Barth sent the sailors' spokesmen to Ebert. Ebert refused to see them.

Now the sailors' patience was at an end. On Dorrenbach's orders they barred all exits from the Reich Chancellery, occupied the telephone exchange and cut the lines. This put the People's Commissars in the Chancellery under house arrest. The sailors could have rounded up the members of the Government, could have arrested and shot the People's Commissars – if they had wanted to. But of course this idea never entered the heads of Dorrenbach and his men. All they wanted was their pay! And they were now really furious. They felt they were getting a rough deal on all sides and did not see why they should have to put up with it.

After all, who had the arms? Who was the stronger? And, when all was said and done, who had made the Revolution? To whom did Fritz Ebert and Otto Wels owe their positions? Now these gentlemen would experience something that would make them think again. They would never again consider it wise to refuse revolutionary sailors their pay!

While one section of the sailors was keeping the People's Commissars locked up in the Reich Chancellery, another, bigger section marched to the City Command. Here they met with resistance. The sentries refused to allow the sailors into the building. A struggle broke out at the gates; then an armoured car appeared outside and fired at the sailors. There were three dead.

Now the sailors attacked the building and took it by storm, arrested Wels and two of his assistants and dragged them to the royal stables. On the way they punched and beat them and threatened them with being put to death. It was of no help to Wels that he now offered them their pay. They took the pay, but they also took him along with them. Meanwhile the People's Commissars remained imprisoned in the Chancellery. It was 5 p.m., in the early December dark.

There was one thing the sailors did not know when they occupied the telephone exchange at the Reich Chancellery and cut the lines; that between Ebert's study and the High Command (now in Kassel) there was a direct line which by-passed the exchange. Ebert now made use of this line to call for help. At the other end of the line was a man who was later to play a major part in events – Major Kurt von Schleicher. On this day he had his first cue-call on to the historical stage. 'I shall arrange at once,' he declared, 'for troops loyal to the Government to be sent from the environs of Berlin for your liberation. Perhaps', he added hopefully, 'there will now, after so many missed opportunities, be a chance to aim a blow at the radicals.'

At the same time as the sailors were returning to the *Marstall* with their pay, secured by force, and with Wels as their prisoner, the High Command gave the order by telephone that units in Potsdam and Babelsberg were to march towards Berlin. They were the last operational remnants of those ten divisions who had been meant to 'create order' in Berlin between December 10 and 15; barely more than eight hundred men, but with a few batteries of field artillery. The sailors, somewhat more than a thousand men, had only machine guns and small arms.

Now the picture gets confused. What happened in the late afternoon of December 23 cannot be clearly reconstructed from the contradictory reports. It is not clear whether the house arrest of the People's Commissars was called off during this time or not; in any case between 5 and 7 p.m. there was a Cabinet meeting, at which Ebert told the three Independents nothing of the approaching troops and after which, at supper time, the Independents left the Chancellery unmolested and suspecting nothing. Ebert and his SPD colleagues stayed inside.

It is not clear either how the sailors came to know of the approaching troops. But somehow they must have found out, for at 8.30 p.m., when the stage gets more clearly lit again, it reveals a martial scene. From two directions heavily armed columns rattle towards the Chancellery: from the West, from the direction of the Tiergarten, the troops from Potsdam and Babelsberg, shouldering their rifles and with horse-drawn field-guns; from the East, from the *Marstall*, the entire People's Naval Division in full marching trim. The sailors get there a little before the soldiers. For the third time that day Dorrenbach calls on Ebert: there were battle-ready troops in the Tiergarten. What was that meant to mean? If they were not withdrawn, fighting would start here and now.

At this point the commanding officers of the summoned troops also enter Ebert's room, make their reports and ask for the order to open fire. The leaders of the two opposing forces stand face to face in front of Ebert whom both, somewhat mistrustfully, regard to some extent as their man. The sailors – for was he not still the People's Commissar of their revolution? The officers – for had he not called them to effect his 'liberation'?

One would give a good deal to have a tape-recording of this scene. Not a word, alas, is known of what was said that evening in Ebert's study. One only knows the result: both sides marched off again, the soldiers back to the Tiergarten, the sailors back to the *Marstall*. It is also known that Ebert promised that the whole affair would be settled the next day by decision of the Cabinet. Meanwhile: no bloodshed!

But it is also known that during the night, at about 2 a.m., Ebert issued an order to the troops encamped in the Tiergarten to attack the *Marstall* in the morning and to round up the People's Naval Division.

There is disagreement about the motives behind this order. The following day Ebert claimed that he had been telephoned from the *Marstall* and told that Otto Wels's life was in danger. This theory is suspect as there is no record that the telephone lines, cut the previous day, had been restored. Nor is the argument convincing; if Wels's life had really been in danger, an attack on the building where he was held was the surest way of bringing about his death. There is also Scheidemann's evidence that early in the morning, at 3 a.m., several hours before the attack took place even if one hour after it was ordered, Wels himself turned up at the Reich Chancellery, much affected by his ordeal but alive and unhurt. Here was another sign of the odd moderation which characterized the German revolutionaries of 1918 even in their moments of rage. No doubt Wels was roughly handled, and there was every intention of giving Ebert and his colleagues a proper fright. But that was all there was to it: nobody wanted to go to extremes. Nobody wanted to commit murder, not even in anger. The counter-Revolution was to have no such scruples.

Another version, which sounds more probable, is that at about midnight there was a serious telephone conversation between General Groener and Ebert, in the course of which Groener threatened to renounce the pact with Ebert if no action was taken.

Ebert probably did not need much persuading. He had been genuinely frightened that afternoon and evening, and fear easily and readily turns to fury. In any case, at 2 a.m. the order to attack was issued from the Chancellery and at 7.45 a.m. the guns thundered on the Schlossplatz.

The battle lasted, with interruptions, until noon and ended in victory for the sailors. That much is certain. Detailed accounts of the course of the encounter are confused and contradictory. The cannonade with which the Ebert troops opened the battle clearly failed in its objective. They fired artillery and machine guns from several sides. During the first hour alone sixty shells hit the palace and *Marstall*. The buildings suffered severe damage but the sailors held their positions.

Between 9 and 10 a.m., with the battle still fierce and un-decided, the gunfire attracted civilians in vast numbers – workers with women and children came pouring out of the side streets; their appearance is said to have had a demoralizing effect on the government troops for they obviously sided with the sailors. The crowd's mood recalled that of November 9: 'Brothers, don't shoot!'

At about ten o'clock there was a pause in the fighting, to get the women and children away from the scene of battle. At 10.30 the fight was resumed with increased intensity, and now it was the sailors' turn to attack. Individual soldiers are said to have crossed over to their side; they were also being reinforced by armed civilians. At any rate, according to a report in the next day's *Vorwärts* (not the kind of paper likely to support the sailors), by noon 'the entire region around the *Marstall* including the Königstrasse as far as the *Rathaus* (Town Hall) was occupied by sailors and their supporters with machine guns'.

At this point the battle finally ceased. The troops who had started it in the morning undertook to clear the battle area and were allowed to depart unmolested. The sailors undertook to return to their quarters – from which they were to have been expelled. They had won the day. Both sides carried off their dead and wounded, whose numbers have remained unknown.

That afternoon there was dismay and deep depression both at

Headquarters in Kassel and in the Chancellery in Berlin. Major von Harbou, who acted as General Staff Officer with the troops in the operation, wired Kassel: 'TROOPS OF THE GENERAL COMMAND LEQUIS CAN NO LONGER BE USED IN ACTION. I SEE NO WAY OF PROTECTING THE GOVERNMENT WITH THE MEANS SO FAR EMPLOYED. THE RESULT OF TODAY'S CLASH CAN BECOME A POLITICAL CATASTROPHE FOR THE GOVERNMENT. THE GENERAL COMMAND LEQUIS HAS BECOME IMPOSSIBLE IN MY VIEW. RECOMMEND ITS DISSOLUTION.' (General Lequis was the Commanding Officer of the ten divisions who had marched into Berlin two weeks earlier.) At a staff conference hurriedly summoned in Kassel several officers expressed themselves in favour of dissolving the High Command. 'It was no use rebelling any longer against fate. Each of them had better travel home and see how he might protect his family and defend his life.'

It was Major von Schleicher who put an end to this defeatism – and thus for the second time in two days intervened in the course of German history. If they did not throw the towel in, he said with prescience, the Berlin defeat would remain a mere episode. Salvation would come from the volunteer battalions now being formed. Groener supported this view. He knew that the *Freikorps* were actively being mustered and he was convinced that time was on the side of the counter-Revolution.

Ebert was less well informed; the High Command took care not to show him its hand. But he was well aware that if the Revolution were to exploit its victory, he would be helpless. He was seriously concerned about a possible attack on the Reich Chancellery and was no doubt worried about his own safety, not without reason.

Groener, who had telephoned him again late on Christmas Eve, describes him as calm, phlegmatic, almost humorous. Asked what he now intended to do, Ebert (according to Groener), replied: 'First of all I shall visit some friends and get some sleep which I badly need. Let Liebknecht occupy the Reich Chancellery if he wants to. He will find the birds have flown.'

Other eye-witnesses who spoke with Ebert that evening, saw a less impressive picture. As during the previous night, and again after the defeat outside the Royal Palace, Ebert, in a state of near panic, is said to have insisted on leaving Berlin together with the entire government – to go anywhere, far out into the quiet of the country, to Rudolstadt or Weimar. 'It cannot go on like this,' he is said to have kept repeating with almost hysterical emphasis. 'One simply cannot govern like this.'

Perhaps Ebert appeared more composed in talking to Groener than in conversation with his colleagues. Both accounts agree that he no longer felt safe in the Chancellery. With things as they were, he had every reason. If the Revolution had not lacked leadership – there would have been nothing, that Christmas Eve, to stop it from taking control of the capital.

But the Revolution had no leadership; it did not see its chance – and also, by now, it was Christmas Eve. The sailors at last had their pay, they had fought and won; now they were intent on celebrating.

As for Karl Liebknecht – who had nothing at all to do with the events of the last few days – he spent the entire night preparing a particularly effective issue of the *Rote Fahne*, the extreme left-wing paper *Red Flag*, which appeared the next morning with a huge banner headline: 'EBERT'S BLOODY CHRISTMAS.' The revolutionary *Obleute*, who, like everyone else, spent that evening around the Christmas tree singing 'Silent Night', called for a demonstration on Christmas Day, with the slogan: 'Situation serious, the Revolution in great danger.' But the Independent Socialists, with Haase melancholy as ever at their head, could see only one thing: they had to leave the Government; they did not wish to be involved in further dreadful events like those which had occurred on December 24 without their knowledge or complicity.

This was probably the biggest favour they could do Ebert and his collaborators. Groener later praised Ebert for cleverly using the Christmas crisis to push the Independents out of the Government; and Walter Oehme, at that time Secretary to the Head of the Reich Chancellery office, reports that even before Christmas there were unmistakable machinations against the three USPD People's Commissars in the Reich Chancellery.

The daily gossip treated their resignations as imminent. Replacements from among the right-wing socialists were already being mooted. If earlier the whole machinery of the Chancellery had been clearly biased in favour of the three right-wing Commissars, from that day onwards (the winding up of the National Congress of Councils and the election of a purely SPD Central Council) it worked for them exclusively. Haase, Dittmann and Barth were slowly being eliminated.

But if this was indeed the case – a few Social Democrat historians deny it – they could have spared themselves the trouble. Haase, Dittmann and Barth, the USPD People's Commissars, eliminated themselves.

Their political tactics during the intra-Governmental controversy about the events of December 23 and 24 were so naïve that one can only explain them by assuming that consciously or unconsciously they had the sole aim of shedding the responsibility of government to which they had not measured up. They spent a whole day fruitlessly arguing with their SPD colleagues about the rights and wrongs of the order to fire issued on December 24 – and then called upon the Central Council, which was manned exclusively by SPD representatives, to arbitrate; and when, as was to be expected, the Central Council decided against them, they resigned from the government.

This took place on December 29. By the next day the three SPD People's Commissars had added to their number two new colleagues from their own party, Wissell and Noske. 'Socialist Unity', proclaimed a bare seven weeks earlier, was buried with undisguised rejoicing. 'The hampering discord is over' they announced cheerfully in a proclamation to the German people, 'Now we have the chance to work!' The proclamation said the aim towards which they would work was 'peace and security'. The word 'revolution' was not mentioned any more. It was signed: 'The Reich Government.' The Council of People's Commissars was abolished.

In this way the Revolution's first and only military victory developed within five days into its decisive political defeat. On November 9 and 10, Ebert, in an effort to halt the Revolution, had been forced to concede a 'Government of Socialist Unity'.

Now, seven weeks later, this Socialist unity – which from the start had been more illusory than real – was at an end. All those political forces which had really favoured or at least sympathized with it, were again excluded. Not that they were blameless: they had missed their moment and failed to grasp their chance. They had been out-manœuvred – or had outmanœuvred themselves.

The immediate and inevitable result was the disintegration of the political Left. After any defeat, the vanquished dispute among themselves; each blames the other for what has happened. This is what they did now.

On December 30 the Spartacists finally broke with the USPD and formed themselves into the Communist Party. At the same time they quarrelled with the revolutionary *Obleute*, who wanted no part in this new creation and who had long thought Liebknecht's 'street tactics' – constant demonstrations – dangerous and amateurish.

Even the congress called to found the Communist Party (KPD) was, from the start, the scene of sharp disagreements between the mass of supporters who clamoured for immediate action, and the leadership who foresaw a long, slow struggle. (Rosa Luxemburg: 'Comrades, you are taking your radicalism somewhat too easily . . . We are at the beginning of the Revolution.')

After the departure of the Spartacists, the USPD remained in a state of schism. Some members of its right-wing were tempted to rejoin the SPD. Its left-wing accused the former People's Commissars of having failed in every way. The revolutionary *Obleute* expelled Emil Barth, the man who had been their only representative in the Council of People's Commissars and who as little as seven weeks earlier had been one of their leaders.

But while the political leadership of the Left disintegrated, the workers, during those Christmas days, evolved a new revolutionary mood. In November the masses had thought they had won. Since Christmas they felt betrayed, cheated of their victory – but not yet defeated. They would have to try once again. Hadn't they managed without leaders in November? If it was possible then, why shouldn't it be possible now?

When, on Sunday, December 29, the burial of those sailors killed in battle took place, a seemingly endless procession of mourners followed them to the Friedrichshain in the East of Berlin. The mourners were angry. There were posters saying:

> Who killed the sailors? Name them we can:
> Ebert, Landsberg and Scheidemann

and:

> Violence against Violence!

They raised their fists and chanted in unison: 'Down with the traitors!'

This rising up and flooding of the streets of East Berlin was the second wave of the Revolution. Within a week it was to break.

Rosa Luxenburg addressing a meeting during the Socialist Congress of 1907. She spent most of the War in prison and was only released on November 9, 1918. Two months later, on January 15, 1919, she was murdered. In 1962 the Federal Government referred to the murders of Luxemburg and Liebknecht as 'executions by shooting under martial law'. (Photo: Ullstein)

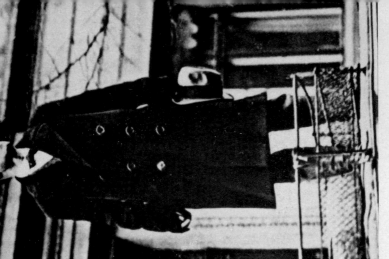

Above l to r: Kurt Eisner, the Berlin Jewish intellectual who led the Revolution in Munich. He was murdered on February 21, 1919. (*Photo: Der Spiegel*) (c) Eugen Leviné, delegated by the Berlin Communist Party to get the Party on its feet in Bavaria. 'Made of the stuff to become a German Lenin or Trotsky', he subsequently took control of the Provisional National Council in Munich, then resigned, and was shot during the ensuing 'White Terror'.

10. Decision in January

The fate of the German Revolution was decided in Berlin during the week of January 5 to 12, 1919. History remembers it as 'Spartacus Week' – but wrongly. What happened that week was not a Communist rising against the Social Democrat Government. It was an attempt by the Berlin workers to regain what they had won on November 9 and 10 and had meanwhile half lost, and to regain it by the same means as before. January 5 was another November 9.

But whereas November at least produced the appearance of success, January brought complete failure. Failure partly because the leadership, again in the hands of the Revolutionary *Obleute*, operated with even less planning and even less skill than the last time. But failure chiefly because Ebert now felt strong enough to risk what he had not dared to do the last time: to have the Revolution stifled.

No one had planned or could have foreseen the events of January 5 in Berlin. It was a spontaneous mass explosion. The occasion was trivial. The Berlin Chief of Police, an insignificant man named Emil Eichhorn, who achieved no kind of prominence either before or afterwards, refused to accept his dismissal by the Prussian Ministry of the Interior. He was a member of the USPD and turned for support to the Berlin section of his Party. On January 4, a Saturday, there was a meeting at Police Headquarters between the executive of the Berlin USPD, the Revolutionary *Obleute* and two representatives from the newly formed KPD, Karl Liebknecht and Wilhelm Pieck. They conferred with Eichhorn and decided to call a protest demonstration against his dismissal, to assemble on Sunday. It was the only action they could envisage; they were to have the surprise of their lives.

The call they sent out was for 'an impressive mass demonstration in the Siegesallee' on Sunday at 2 p.m. But already, during the morning, as on November 9, huge columns of workers came flooding from all the working-class suburbs into the city centre. By two o'clock, hundreds of thousands were standing shoulder to shoulder, not only in the Siegesallee, but right across the Tiergarten, along Unter den Linden, on the Schlossplatz, and from there down the Königstrasse to the Alexanderplatz where Police Headquarters were situated.

It was not a peaceful gathering. On the contrary, it was a show of strength. Many were armed; all were angry and eager for action. After listening to speeches – which most of them could not hear for in those days there were no loudspeakers – the masses did not disperse. Just as on November 9 a few courageous people suddenly took the initiative, issued instructions and assembled in armed groups and columns. After all, they did not merely want to demonstrate, they wanted to act – to do something.

Later it was claimed that Government spies were involved as *agents provocateurs*. This is not impossible but they would not have been able to incite the crowd to the sort of action that followed if the people involved had not already been bent on such action.

In the course of the afternoon the demonstration had turned into an armed operation. Its main target was the newspaper district. All the big newspaper publishing houses – Scherl, Ullstein, Mosse, *Vorwärts* – were occupied, the presses stopped, the editorial staffs sent home. Later other armed groups occupied the major railway stations.

During the night excited columns were still roaming through the centre of Berlin, looking for strategic points to occupy or resistance to overcome. But there was no resistance. The Revolution which had lain dormant since November 10 had again erupted. That night it appeared to have taken control of Berlin.

No one was more surprised by this universal eruption than the people who had triggered it off. They had had no idea of the avalanche they were unleashing.

On this Sunday evening eighty-six men were assembled in the Berlin Police Headquarters: seventy Revolutionary *Obleute*, ten members of the executive of the Berlin USPD led by the ageing Georg Ledebour, two soldiers' and one sailors' representative, Liebknecht and Pieck as delegates of the KPD and, finally, Eichhorn himself. According to the report of a participant, the conference was 'completely under the spell of the tremendous demonstration without at first coming to any conclusions as to what was to happen next'. A mood prevailed 'which permitted no objective analysis. The speakers vied with one another in their demands and their invective.'

Wilder than most was Heinrich Dorrenbach, the leader of the People's Naval Division, who was not only intoxicated like all the others by the overwhelming impressions of the last few hours, but was still swollen with the victory in the Christmas battle. He now claimed that 'not only the People's Naval Division, but all the other Berlin regiments are backing the Revolutionary *Obleute* and are ready to overthrow the Ebert–Scheidemann Government by force of arms'. Whereupon Liebknecht said that in this case the overthrow of the Government was possible and absolutely necessary. Ledebour said: 'If we decide on that, we must move quickly.'

The two soldiers' representatives uttered words of warning. 'Perhaps the troops *are* behind us,' one of them said, 'but they have always vacillated.' The other was more pessimistic still. It was even questionable, he said, whether Dorrenbach had the backing of his own men (a doubt which was all too soon to prove well-founded). But the warnings could not prevail against the intoxication of victory which, oddly enough, had not been imparted to the masses by their leaders, but had swept from the masses into the leadership. By 80 votes to 6 it was decided 'to take up the fight against the Government and carry it on until its overthrow'.

The same night the following proclamation was issued:

Workers! Soldiers! Comrades! On Sunday you displayed with overwhelming power your determination to thwart the last evil-minded plot of the bloodstained Ebert Government. Now bigger issues are at stake. We must put a stop to all counter-revolutionary machinations! Therefore come out of the factories! Assemble in vast numbers this morning in the Siegesallee at 11 a.m.! The Revolution must be implemented and strengthened! Up and into battle for Socialism! Up and into battle for the power of the Revolutionary proletariat! Down with the Ebert–Scheidemann Government!

A 'provisional Revolutionary Committee' was formed with no less than fifty-three members, headed by Ledebour, Liebknecht and a certain Paul Scholze; this Revolutionary Committee declared that it had 'provisionally taken over the business of government'. In fact it never took over the business of government or even of the Revolution. The proclamation for the renewed mass gathering on Monday was all it ever achieved.

This proclamation was obeyed. On Monday morning the masses were again in the streets, in perhaps even greater numbers than on Sunday. Shoulder to shoulder they again stood from the Siegesallee to the Alexanderplatz, armed, expectant, ready for action. They now felt strong. Yesterday they had, almost playfully, shown their strength and power – quite spontaneously, unled. Now that they thought they had leadership, they expected determination, battle and victory.

And then nothing happened. The leadership remained silent. Individual groups again went off on their own and occupied a few more public buildings – the Wolff Telegraph Office and the Government Printing Office among them. Evidently nobody was ready to attempt a decisive assault on the Government buildings without being given the order – and no order came. Also there were a few thousand Government supporters massed outside the Chancellery, armed civilians drummed up by the SPD that morning.

The hours passed. The day which had begun with beautiful winter sunshine grew foggy, then unpleasantly wet and cold. Slowly darkness fell. And no order came. The sandwiches had been eaten and hunger returned, the everlasting hunger of this winter of revolution. By the end of the afternoon the masses slowly began to thin out. By evening they had dispersed. When midnight struck, the centre of Berlin lay deserted. Although no

one was as yet aware of it, on this January 6, 1919 the German
Revolution had died.

What had happened? Above all it was this: the hoped-for
support of the troops for this second wave of revolution had failed
to materialize. The soldiers' representative's warning of the
previous evening was proved right. The troops hesitated, debated,
did not quite know what was going on; as usual they were in
favour both of revolution and of law and order. At any rate, they
felt no inclination to risk their necks. Even the People's Naval
Division opted for 'neutrality'. In the morning, the fifty-three-
man Revolutionary Committee had transferred, full of hope,
from Police Headquarters to the *Marstall*, the sailors' headquarters. In the afternoon they were politely shown the door.
And thus they had spent their day.

In the evening there was again a meeting at Police Headquarters,
but now there was a very different mood. It was no longer a
question of how to overthrow the Government, but merely of
how to get out of the whole business with impunity.

On this Monday evening this still seemed possible, as it did
for the next two or three days. During this time, both sides were
wary of each other; the Government as much as the revolutionaries. The former were still sweating from Sunday's
experience, and on Monday another gigantic crowd could clearly
be seen to be forming from the Wilhelmstrasse; the Linden, a
hundred yards away, resembled an armed camp: what would
happen if this army launched an attack on the Government
buildings? The true helplessness of the revolutionary leadership
was not yet evident. And the majority of the Berlin troops were
not to be relied on: by the Government as little as by the
revolutionaries.

True, the *Freikorps*, the volunteer units, were getting ready on
the provincial parade grounds outside Berlin. On Saturday,
Ebert and Noske had been to Zossen to inspect the newly formed
Landesjägerkorps under General Maercker and had been agreeably
surprised at seeing 'real soldiers' again. Noske, the taller by two
heads, had patted Ebert on the shoulder and said: 'Cheer up,
everything will be alright soon.' But that had been Saturday in

Zossen; now it was Monday in Berlin, and it was not the *Landesjägerkorps* massed in the Unter den Linden, but the armed revolution.

It was therefore a welcome relief when the former USPD People's Commissars, who had left the Government on December 29, now offered to mediate. Ebert was happy to accept. At the very least it was a way to gain time. He made only one condition: the occupation of the newspaper offices must cease.

This condition was debated by the Revolutionary Committee on Monday evening. If they had agreed to it, the situation might still have been saved. But they said no.

This paralytic monster of a committee was a pitiful sight from first to last: incapable of advancing, unwilling to retreat. After yesterday's victorious delirium the mood had crashed too steeply. To recognize and admit defeat, to beat a retreat, was more than these fifty-three men could psychologically accomplish within twenty-four hours.

Perhaps they also had secret doubts about whether they could in fact guarantee the evacuation of the newspaper offices. They had not ordered them to be occupied and had no power over the armed groups in the newspaper buildings; in many cases they did not even know who was in command. In fact, in this Revolution, the Revolutionary Committee at Police Headquarters played the part of the simpleton. But that had to be kept dark. They said no.

At heart, Ebert was content. He wanted no repetition of that illusory peace pact with the Revolution as on November 10; he wanted the pay-off. ('The day of reckoning approaches!' says a Government proclamation formulated by him and issued two days later, on January 8.) He protracted the inauspicious negotiations for a few days and made his military preparations. They were two-pronged.

One prong was Noske, with the *Freikorps*. As recently as Monday, in the half-besieged Chancellery, Noske had been appointed Commander-in-Chief. ('It is all right by me,' he remarked according to his own testimony. 'Someone has got to be the bloodhound.') He had immediately left the danger-zone, passing freely through the armed crowd at the Brandenburg

Gate who had no idea who the tall, bespectacled civilian was. ('I repeatedly asked politely to be let through. I had an urgent errand, I said. They readily made way for me.') Since then he had established himself in the West Berlin suburb of Dahlem, in the *Luisenstift*, a smart girls' boarding school enjoying extended Christmas holidays. There he had made his headquarters, and from there he busied himself with mustering the new *Freikorps* around Berlin and preparing their march into the city. In Dahlem there was no sign of revolution, no worker roamed that far. In the spacious, wintry gardens there was a gracious peace. Noske could work undisturbed. But his work needed time and Ebert had none. There was still a general strike in Berlin, the newspapers and railway stations were still occupied, the Revolutionary Committee was still in session at Police Headquarters, there were still vast mass demonstrations in the East and North of the city. If the *Freikorps* were not yet ready to march – could not something after all be done with the Berlin troops? Ebert was willing to try. It should be possible to employ some unit or other against the Spartacists, for God's sake!

This was the second prong he sharpened against the Revolution, while still negotiating and expressing his disapproval of bloodshed. And in fact the Berlin troops finally tilted the scales. When the *Freikorps* moved into Berlin at last, the battle had been fought.

The days of battle were Thursday, January 9 to Sunday January 12, 1919. During this period, on Ebert's orders, the Revolution in the capital was mown down with gunfire. Day after day Berliners heard the roar of cannon, previously heard only on December 24. A motley assembly of troops – the ever-conservative 'May-Bugs' (*Maikäfer*), the newly-formed Reichstag Regiment, loyal to Ebert, the right-wing radical volunteer regiment *Reinhard* which had been put together during the days of Christmas, and finally the Potsdam battalions under Major von Stephani, reorganized after their ignominious defeat on Christmas Eve – fought violent street and house-to-house battles to retake the occupied buildings one by one, including, finally, the Police Headquarters building on Sunday.

The fiercest battle raged on Saturday morning, January 11,

around the *Vorwärts* building in the Lindenstrasse. The first gun
salvo failed, as it had done in the fight for the Palace, the first
assault was repelled; then there followed a second, more powerful
salvo and then a dreadful thing happened. The *Vorwärts* garrison
sent out six spokesmen bearing a white flag to negotiate a safe
conduct. One of them was sent back with a demand for un-
conditional surrender, the remaining five were kept behind,
taken away, brutally maltreated and finally shot, together with
two captured couriers. The *Vorwärts* was then taken by storm.
Three hundred of the defenders were taken captive.

Major von Stephani telephoned the Reich Chancellery to ask
what he was to do with so many prisoners. According to his own
written testimony, he received the reply: 'Shoot the lot!' This he
refused to do; he was still an officer of the old school. Seven of the
prisoners were shot nevertheless and almost all were cruelly
beaten with gun-butts, without von Stephani being able to
prevent it. A Government archivist, *Reichsarchivrat* Volkmann,
who has written a history of the Revolution which tends throughout to side with the military, reports as follows:

In their rage the soldiers are almost out of control. When they see how
one of the officers, who had been captured by the rebels and held
prisoner in the *Vorwärts* building during the bombardment, shook the
Spartacists by the hand to thank them for their considerate treatment
of him, they beat him till he bled.

On January 12 the fighting in Berlin was over. The Revolution
had been crushed. Had it been a Spartacist, that is to say a
Communist revolution? The victors said so from the start, and
their nomenclature has prevailed to the present day. (Note the
unquestioning conviction with which Volkmann calls the occu-
pants of the *Vorwärts* 'Spartacists'.)

But this is not the truth. The KPD had neither foreseen nor
desired the January rising, they had neither planned nor guided it.
They were in fact horrified by the unplanned, leaderless, mass
stampede. Such a massed rising, when the Party had barely found
its feet, was against all the rules! When, on January 8, Liebknecht
after some days of absence turned up at the Party headquarters,

he was showered with reproaches for having taken it upon himself to participate. 'Karl, is that our programme?' Rosa Luxemburg is said to have shouted out to him; or, according to another version: 'Karl, what has happened to our programme?'

And even the lamentable Revolutionary Committee – on which it was not the two Communists, Liebknecht and Pieck, who called the tune, but the seventy Revolutionary *Obleute* – had neither planned, caused nor led the January rising. This rising had been the exclusive and spontaneous doing of the Berlin working masses, the same masses who had produced the November Revolution and who were overwhelmingly Social Democrat, not Spartacist or Communist, and whose rising in January had not differed from that in November.

There is evidence for this, for the masses did not remain silent. In the second half of that tragic week in January, when they too had realized the failure of the 'Revolutionary Committee' and when the cannons were already speaking in the newspaper district, they formulated their aims in the course of big mass demonstrations, and did so with remarkable clarity.

On January 9 – Thursday – forty thousand workers of the AEG and the *Schwarzkopf* works assembled in the Humboldthain, called – just as on November 10 – for the 'unity of workers of all persuasions' and instituted a commission on which the Socialist factions were equally represented. In the days that followed the unity movement affected practically all Berlin's factories. The Four Points Resolution passed by the Spandau factories (eighty thousand workers) on January 10 is typical:

1 The resignation of all People's Commissars
2 Formation of evenly-balanced committees of the three Parties
3 New elections for the workers' and soldiers' councils, the central council, the executive council and the People's Commissars
4 Setting about the unification of the socialist parties

Equally characteristic was the demand voiced by the workers in the electricity plants *Südwest, Schöneberg*, on January 11 – Friday – for the resignation of 'leaders of *all political persuasions* who have proved incapable of preventing this terrible fratricide'.

5*

These are not Spartacist or Communist aims. They are the very aims to which Ebert had paid lip-service on November 10: Socialist unity, 'no fratricide'. They are the aims for which the workers of Berlin had fought on November 9, and for these aims they had once again, spontaneously and without leadership, taken up arms in that gory week of January.

They still wanted what they had wanted in November: the unification of all Socialist parties and the abolition of the old feudal-bourgeois State in favour of a new workers' State. Ebert on November 10 had pretended to grant this. But it had never been his wish: from the start he was eager to preserve the old structure. And this is what the workers of Berlin realized between November and January; and that is why in January they produced, not a Spartacist or Communist revolution, but the same revolution all over again. But if the first time there had been at least an illusion of victory – this time the Revolution ended in bloody defeat.

The workers who had stormed into the streets on November 9 and on January 5 and who, on January 9, 10 and 11 had formulated their aims in mass resolutions, still largely voted Social Democrat during the elections for a Constituent National Assembly a week later. They still considered themselves Social Democrats – not Independents or Communists. In their eyes the people who were no longer Social Democrats were Ebert, Scheidemann and Noske.

But it was Ebert, Scheidemann and Noske who now held power and who decided who from now on was entitled to call himself a Social Democrat and who was to put up with being called 'Spartacist'. They also had the power simply to consign all the workers' resolutions of that January week to the wastepaper basket.

Of course, in order to hold their own supporters in check, they now had to find strange allies – allies inclined to view them as semi-Spartacists themselves. With the same lack of suspicion with which the Revolution two months ago had placed itself in Ebert's hands, Ebert now delivered himself into the hands of the Counter-Revolution.

When Ebert had won his battle for Berlin, Noske, too, had

completed his preparations. The first *Freikorps* were ready to march into Berlin. On Saturday, January 11, after the storming of the *Vorwärts* – there was a foretaste: a demonstration march by the *Landesjägerkorps Maercker* through bourgeois West Berlin. The conservative *Post* reported it the next day under the headline 'A GLEAM OF LIGHT':

Yesterday afternoon at about three o'clock many a patriotic heart could once again rejoice at a long-missed sight. Soldiers were marching across the Potsdamer Platz in the direction of the Dönhoffplatz. Soldiers with officers, soldiers controlled by their leaders. An immense crowd lined both sides and welcomed them with enthusiastic cheers. The march stopped, the troops were forced to halt. Sharp commands of 'Company halt! Slope arms!' were executed with disciplined precision. Shouts of 'Bravo!' from the public. All were looking with admiration at this first-class, impeccable, disciplined unit and its leaders.

What the *Post* failed to report was that this first-class unit had marching at its head a lonely, tall, bespectacled civilian: Gustav Noske. This was a moment he was not prepared to miss. Volkmann, quoted above, has a snapshot of the strange picture: 'The deadly serious face betrays an iron will. At his side, half mocking, half embarrassed, a colonel.'

This march was a mere prelude. On January 15, the Wednesday after the week of revolution, the whole South and West of Berlin and the City Centre were occupied by the newly-formed 'General Command Lüttwitz'. The North and East – the workers' districts – were for the time being excluded. Their subjection, when bloodshed would be inevitable, was left for later.

The West of Berlin was taken over by the newly-formed *Garde-Kavallerie-Schützendivision*. They established their headquarters in the palatial Eden Hotel. They brought posters along which read: 'The *Garde-Kavallerie-Schützendivision* has marched into Berlin. Berliners! The Division promises you not to leave the Capital until order has finally been re-established.'

On the very day of its arrival the division left its visiting card: by murdering Karl Liebknecht and Rosa Luxemburg.

11. The Persecution and Murder of Karl Liebknecht and Rosa Luxemburg

When on the evening of January 15, 1919, Karl Liebknecht and Rosa Luxemburg, beaten senseless with rifle-butts, were taken by car from the Eden Hotel in Berlin to the Tiergarten to be murdered, the course of political events was at first pretty well unaffected. The Revolution's last hour had already struck; Liebknecht had only played a very peripheral part in it, Rosa Luxemburg had not taken any active part at all. In any case, the Revolution was about to be brutally crushed. The murder of the two figures that symbolized it perhaps helped to give the signal for the massacre; in the overall course of events this crime seemed at the time to be no more than a garish episode.

Today one realizes with horror that this episode was historically the most potent event in the drama of the German Revolution. Viewed from the vantage point of half a century later, it has acquired something of the uncanny, incalculably far-reaching effect of the event on Golgotha – which likewise seemed to make little difference when it happened.

Death brought Liebknecht and Rosa Luxemburg together. During their lives they had had little in common until right at the very end. They had very different careers and were totally different personalities.

Liebknecht was one of the most courageous men Germany has ever produced. He was not a great politician. Before 1914 he was hardly known outside the SPD; and inside the Party he counted for little – the insignificant son of a great father, Wilhelm Liebknecht, the Party's founder: 'a hot-headed, obstinate lawyer with a kind heart and a weakness for the dramatic.'

He had worked with young people and written a book against militarism which earned him eighteen months of imprisonment; it was only then that the Party, half as a gesture of defiance, half as a consolation prize, chose him as an election candidate; from 1908 onwards he was in the Prussian Regional Parliament (*Landtag*); from 1912 onwards he was in the Reichstag, the National Assembly. Rosa Luxemburg left a fairly ironic description of Liebknecht as a representative: 'All day in Parliament, at meetings, on committees, at discussions, in a constant rush, always off somewhere, from a train into a tram and from a tram into a car, every pocket crammed with notebooks, his arms loaded with freshly bought newspapers which he would never find time to read, body and soul covered with the dust of the streets . . .' Even as late as the outbreak of the War, when she was trying to bring together within the Party a group in opposition to the War, she wrote: 'One can hardly get hold of Karl because he darts about like a cloud in the air.'

Rosa Luxemburg, on the other hand, had been a political figure of the first rank in Germany since the turn of the century – although a triple outsider, as a woman, a Jewess and a semi-foreigner (she was born in Russian Poland and had only become a German by a fictitious marriage); in addition she terrified the bourgeoisie, and even the Social Democrats, because of her radical views. And yet admired by friends and enemies – often reluctantly – for a multiplicity of talents bordering on genius: a brilliant and penetrating mind, a scintillating style, infectious oratory; a politician through and through and at the same time an original thinker, a warm-hearted, fascinating woman into the bargain. Her wit and her graceful gravity, her passion and kindness made one forget that she was not good-looking. She was loved as much as she was feared and hated.

She had always been at the forefront of the great national and international socialist controversies at the beginning of the century. As their ally or opponent, she was the peer of Bebel and Kautsky, Lenin and Trotsky, Jaurès and Pilsudski. She ventured into the Russian Revolution of 1905 – and again and again she ended up in prison, for *lèse-majesté*, for incitement to disobedience, for insults to the officers' corps. A woman beyond grasp, a great woman, perhaps still the greatest woman this century has produced.

Then suddenly the War changed everything, in a manner recalling *Faust*:

> . . . it takes a woman a thousand paces
> however much she runs or races –
> a man can do it in a single bound.

During the War the unknown backbencher Karl Liebknecht overtook the great Rosa Luxemburg and achieved world fame, not through some act of special political brilliance or intellectual originality, but simply through two acts of courage, immense, single-handed, moral courage. On December 2, 1914 he alone in the Reichstag voted against a second war loan – one must know the mood then prevailing in Germany and the German Reichstag to comprehend what that meant. And on May 1, 1916, during a May demonstration on the Potsdamer Platz in Berlin (not a big demonstration; a few hundred people, at most a thousand, surrounded by police), he began his speech with the words: 'Down with the war! Down with the Government!' He got no further. Policemen overwhelmed him and dragged him off. For the next two and a half years he was out of sight behind prison walls. But those eight words had had more effect than the longest or most brilliant speech. When Liebknecht was set free on October 23, 1918, he had become, for Germany and far beyond her borders, the very embodiment of protest against the War and the embodiment of revolution.

Rosa Luxemburg did not leave prison until November 9, 1918. She had spent almost the entire war behind bars: to start with, one year as the result of a pre-war political verdict, then two and a half years in 'preventive detention'. Those years, during which she had composed her classic critiques of German Social Democracy and of the Russian Revolution, had turned her hair grey, but her mind had lost nothing of its sparkling mastery.

From now on the two of them had a good two months to live, the two months in which the German Revolution broke out and foundered.

If one asks what was Liebknecht's and Rosa Luxemburg's contribution to the drama of these two months, the honest answer must be: little or nothing. Everything would have happened exactly as it did if they had not existed. Even such ephemeral figures as the sailors Artelt and Dorrenbach had, at moments, a greater effect on events than the two great revolutionaries. The real protagonists were Ebert and his crew, the Revolutionary *Obleute*, the sailors, the Berlin troops, the Socialist Party organizations, the council congresses and the masses continually and unpredictably intervening in the action – and on none of these did Luxemburg and Liebknecht have any real influence. Liebknecht made a few appearances on the stage; Rosa Luxemburg none at all.

What they did during these sixty-seven days can be reconstructed in detail. They founded and edited, against many obstacles and under much difficulty, a newspaper, *Die Rote Fahne* (*The Red Flag*), and wrote its daily leading articles. They took part – unsuccessfully – in the meetings and gatherings of the Revolutionary *Obleute* and of the Berlin USPD. Finally, faced with this lack of success, they decided to found their own party, prepared the founding meeting of the KPD, held it, made the main speeches; Rosa Luxemburg drafted the party programme. But this founding congress, too, brought them no personal successes: on important issues they were outvoted. This was during the very last days of 1918. Then, off his own bat, Liebknecht, from January 4, 1919 onwards, took part in the unproductive meetings of the fifty-three-man Revolutionary Committee in the Berlin Police Headquarters. During that time Rosa Luxemburg edited the *Rote Fahne* alone. And then the little of life left to them was already exhausted.

If one also takes into account participation in demonstrations, speeches made off-the-cuff on these occasions, endless discussions with others of the same persuasion, one gets a picture of a more than full period, hectic and short of sleep. In those days from November 9 to January 15, in what remained of their lives, Liebknecht and Rosa Luxemburg worked like people possessed, to the very limits of their strength: but they effected nothing. They were not the leaders of a German Bolshevist revolution, not Germany's Lenin and Trotsky. They did not even seek to be this: Rosa Luxemburg because she rejected the violent element in Lenin and Trotsky's revolution-by-forceps-delivery on grounds of principle, and kept repeating almost solemnly that the Revolution would have to grow naturally and democratically out of the consciousness of the proletarian masses, which in Germany was still in its early beginnings; Liebknecht because he was convinced that the Revolution would make itself, indeed had already done so, and required no further organization or manipulation. Lenin, in April 1917 when he had only just returned to Russia, issued the instruction: 'Organization, organization and more organization!' Liebknecht and Luxemburg did not organize anything. Liebknecht's watchword was: Agitation; Rosa Luxemburg's was: Enlightenment.

And enlighten she did, with daily articles in the *Rote Fahne*. From the outset there was no one to rival Rosa Luxemburg for the accuracy with which she analysed the nature of the German Revolution and the reasons for its failure: the SPD's lack of sincerity, the USPD's lack of purpose, the Revolutionary *Obleute*'s lack of ideas. She did it with penetration, openly and in public. In its own way it was magnificent. But it was a journalistic, not a revolutionary achievement. All that Rosa Luxemburg accomplished by this was to make herself the object of the deadly hatred of those she saw through and exposed.

From the very start this hatred was, quite literally, deadly. There is evidence that the murder of Liebknecht and Rosa Luxemburg was planned and systematically pursued from the beginning of December, if not earlier. In those early December days hoardings throughout Berlin displayed posters which read:

Workers, Citizens! The Fatherland is on the brink of disaster. Save it! It is threatened not from without but from within: by the Spartacist group. Beat their leaders to death! Kill Liebknecht! Then you will have peace, work and bread!

The Front-line Soldiers.

At that time there were, as yet, no front-line soldiers in Berlin. The call for murder came from a different source. We have some indication of the nature of this source. A certain Anton Fischer, who was then deputy to Otto Wels, the City Commander, wrote in 1920 that in November and December of 1918 it had been the policy of his office to 'dig out and hunt down' Liebknecht and Luxemburg 'by day and by night, so that they had no chance to agitate or organize'. As early as the night of December 9 to 10, soldiers of the Second Regiment of Guards forced their way into the building where the *Rote Fahne* was being edited, with the intention – subsequently admitted – of murdering Liebknecht. During the court hearings which followed this event half a dozen witnesses stated that at that time there was already a price of 50,000 marks on the heads of both Liebknecht and Rosa Luxemburg, offered by Scheidemann and Georg Sklarz, a *nouveau-riche* war millionaire who was a close friend of Scheidemann's.

On January 13, 1919, two days before the assassination, the information sheet of the volunteer auxiliary corps in Berlin (*Mitteilungsblatt der freiwilligen Hilfskorps in Berlin*) had this to say:

'The fear has been voiced that the Government might slacken in its action against the Spartacists. Authoritative sources confirm that what has been achieved so far is by no means considered sufficient, and that every effort will be made to act against the leaders of the movement. The population of Berlin should not feel that those who have for the time being got away can live elsewhere in peace. The very next days will show that they, too, will not be spared.'

On the same day the Social Democrat *Vorwärts* published a poem ending with this stanza:

> Many hundred dead in a row –
> Proletarians!
> Karl, Rosa, Radek and Company –
> Not one of them there, not one of them there!
> Proletarians!

A few days earlier in the *Luisenstift* in Dahlem, Gustav Noske, Ebert's civil war Commander-in-Chief, had personally ordered Lieutenant Friedrich Wilhelm von Oertzen to monitor Liebknecht's telephone day and night. Oertzen, who later wrote down a record of all this, was to report all Liebknecht's movements, day by day and hour by hour, to Captain Pabst of the *Garde-Kavallerie-Schützendivision*. It was this order which led to Liebknecht's and Rosa Luxemburg's capture, and Pabst headed the murder squad.

In the end Liebknecht and Rosa Luxemburg can hardly have failed to realize that they were being hunted. It is remarkable and characteristic – in an honourable sense – that even so, not for a moment did it occur to them to leave Berlin; and they refused their supporters' repeated offer of a bodyguard. They were much too involved in their political and journalistic work to spend much time thinking about their own safety; perhaps they were also over-confident – arrest and imprisonment were familiar experiences that held no terror. This very familiarity may have made it difficult for them to realize that this time their lives were really in danger. When she was 'arrested' Rosa Luxemburg touchingly packed a small suitcase with a few belongings and favourite books which had more than once accompanied her into prison.

And yet a kind of fatal foreboding invaded their last days. It had been a breathless period throughout; they had hardly seen their homes during those sixty-seven days; rationing their sleep, they had spent restless nights in the editorial office, in hotel rooms or in the apartments of friends. But this constant change of address took on a new meaning in the last week of their lives – it smacked of flight, of rushing from one inadequate cover to the next, and in a terrible way anticipated the fate of Jews hunted to death in the Third Reich.

The editorial office of the *Rote Fahne*, at the lower end of the Wilhelmstrasse, had become unsafe. Government troops entered it almost daily; one woman editor, whom they mistook for Rosa Luxemburg, narrowly escaped death. For some days Rosa Luxemburg did her editorial work in a doctor's apartment near the Hallesche Tor; then, after her presence had become a burden for her hosts, in a worker's flat in Neukölin. There she was joined on January 12 by Karl Liebknecht, but two days later – on January 14 – a telephoned alert drove them both away (it was perhaps a fake call from the murderers' switchboard which had been shadowing, and possibly even controlling, their every movement for days).

They transferred to their last hideout, to Wilmersdorf, near the Fehrbelliner Platz: Mannheimer Strasse 53, c/o Markussohn. There on the morning of January 15 they wrote their last articles for the *Rote Fahne*. It seems more than just chance that they read like parting words of farewell.

Rosa Luxemburg's article was entitled 'Order prevails in Berlin'. It ends:

O you thick-skulled myrmidons of the law! Your 'order' is built on sand. By tomorrow the Revolution will rise clanking to its feet again and to your horror announce with a fanfare of trumpets: I was. I am. I shall be!

Liebknecht's article 'In spite of Everything' ends thus:

Today's vanquished will be tomorrow's victors . . . Whether or not we shall still be alive when this is achieved – our programme will live on: it will dominate the world of liberated humanity. In spite of everything!

Towards evening – Rosa Luxemburg had a headache and had gone to lie down, and Wilhelm Pieck had just arrived with the galley proofs of the *Rote Fahne* – the doorbell rang. An innkeeper named Mehring was at the door, asking for Herr Liebknecht and Frau Luxemburg. At first their presence was denied, but Mehring persisted. He summoned a group of soldiers led by a Lieutenant Lindner, who searched the flat, found them and asked them to come along. They packed a few things. Then they were taken to the Eden Hotel, which from that morning had been serving as Headquarters of the *Garde-Kavallerie-Schützendivision*. There they were being awaited. The rest happened quickly and is quickly told.

In the Eden Hotel they were greeted with insults and maltreated. Liebknecht, who had been beaten with rifle-butts had two open wounds on his head and asked for bandages, but was refused. He also asked to be allowed to go to the lavatory; that too was refused. They were then both taken to the first floor, to the room of Captain Pabst who was in charge. It is not known what was said in that room. We only have Pabst's own statement in court – which has been shown to have been false on other points –

according to which his conversation with Rosa Luxemburg went as follows:

'Are you Frau Rosa Luxemburg?'

'Please make up your own mind about that.'

'To judge by your pictures, you must be.'

'If you say so.'

Then Liebknecht, and a little later Rosa Luxemburg, were subjected to renewed maltreatment while being taken or dragged down the stairs and handed over to the murder squad, held in readiness. Meanwhile Pabst sat in his room and prepared an extensive report which appeared in all the newspapers the following day. Liebknecht, it read, had been shot while trying to escape when he was being transported to the Moabit prison, while Rosa Luxemburg had been snatched from her escort by an enraged crowd and dragged off to an unknown destination.

In fact the road outside the side exit, through which Karl Liebknecht and Rosa Luxemburg were taken on their last journey, had been barred and was deserted. A Fusilier called Runge had been posted by this side exit. As first Liebknecht, then Rosa Luxemburg were escorted outside, his orders were to smash their heads in with the butt of his rifle. He did as he was told: two vicious blows, but neither of them fatal. Stunned or half-stunned by those terrible blows, Liebknecht, and a few minutes later Rosa Luxemburg, were dragged into cars which were standing by. Liebknecht's murder escort was under the command of a Lieutenant-Captain von Pflugk-Harttung, Rosa Luxemburg's under that of a Lieutenant Vogel.

Within a few minutes of each other both cars drove to the Tiergarten. At the Neue See, a lake, Liebknecht was asked to get out, shot in the back of the head with a pistol, thrown back into the car and then delivered to the mortuary as the 'body of an unknown man'.

Rosa Luxemburg was shot through the temple immediately after being driven away from the Hotel Eden and at the Lichtenstein Bridge was thrown into the Landwehrkanal. It has not been ascertained whether she was killed by being beaten to death, by the bullet or by drowning. When months later the corpse was washed up, the post-mortem showed that the cranium had not been split, the bullet wound had not necessarily been fatal.

Why were Karl Liebknecht and Rosa Luxemburg persecuted and murdered? The legend – carefully nurtured by the Social Democrats, involuntarily supported by the Communists in exaggerating the Spartacist part in the Revolution – obstinately keeps on repeating that they became the victims of a civil war they themselves had unleashed. As far as Rosa Luxemburg is concerned, not a word of this is true. And even if Liebknecht's participation in the Revolutionary Committee of January 1919 were to be regarded as an act of civil war; how is one to explain that nothing happened to the other fifty-two participants, that while Georg Ledebour, who had been every bit as involved and had been arrested on January 10, was acquitted during the subsequent hearings, Liebknecht's persecution had begun early in December, when nobody as yet had any idea of January's impending events? No, the persecution and murder of Karl Liebknecht and Rosa Luxemburg were not acts of combat in the civil war. Other reasons lay behind them.

One reason was that Liebknecht and Rosa Luxemburg, more than anyone else, *embodied* the German Revolution in the eyes of both friends and enemies. They were its symbols, and who killed them, killed the Revolution. This applies to Liebknecht even more than to Rosa Luxemburg.

The other reason was, that, more than anyone else, they saw through the double game which its alleged leaders were playing with the German Revolution, and every day shouted their findings from the rooftops. They were expert witnesses who had to be killed because their testimony was irrefutable. This applies to Rosa Luxemburg even more than it does to Karl Liebknecht.

The murder of Karl Liebknecht and Rosa Luxemburg meant the murdering of a superior courage and a superior spirit. It meant murdering the irrefutable truth.

Who was guilty of this act? The immediate guilt, of course, rests on Captain Pabst, who decades later, in 1962, protected by the Statute of Limitations, openly boasted of his deed, and on his murder squads. They were all surely more than mere tools, dully and indifferently executing orders; they acted willingly, even eagerly. But were they alone, or even directly, responsible? It must be remembered that the persecution, the public incitement to murder, and the preparations for the murder itself began at the latest in the beginning of December 1918, long before the murderers from the *Garde-Kavallerie-Schützendivision* entered the stage. One must remember the price on their heads, the testimony of the Berlin Deputy City Commander, the unmistakable incitement to murder, not only in the conservative press, but also and especially in the Social Democrat papers; and after the event, Scheidemann's hypocritical defence, Noske's cold satisfaction. Ebert, as far as can be ascertained, always kept silent as the grave.

One must also remember the undisguised, indeed shameless manner in which judiciary and Government authorities favoured the actual murderers. (Most of them were acquitted in the course of farcical proceedings at a court martial of their own division even those who received minor sentences for 'dereliction of sentry duty' and 'body-snatching'; they were immediately afterwards helped to escape.) And finally one must remember the reaction of bourgeois and Social Democrat public opinion, ranging from whitewashing understatement to open rejoicing: a hypocritical reaction which remains unchanged to the present day.

As recently as 1954 the liberal lawyer and historian Erich Eyck wrote:

One does not excuse the murder if one recalls the old adage that he who lives by the sword shall perish by the sword, and one has witnessed too many bloody deeds by those who think like Liebknecht and like Rosa Luxemburg to feel especially outraged at their fate.

And as late as 1962 the *Bulletin des Presse- und Informationsamtes der Bundesregierung Nr 27* (Handout No. 27 from the Press and Information Office of the German Federal Government) called the murders 'executions by shooting under martial law'.

The murders of January 15, 1919 were a prelude – the prelude to murders by the thousand in the following months under Noske, and to murders by the million in the ensuing decades under Hitler. They were the starting signal for all the others. Yet this one crime remains unadmitted, unexpiated and unrepented. That is why it still cries out to heaven in Germany. That is why its light sears the German present like a lethal laser beam.

12. The Civil War

From January to May 1919, with off-shoots reaching into the height of summer, a bloody civil war was waged in Germany, leaving in its wake thousands of dead, and unspeakable bitterness.

This civil war set the points for the unhappy history of the Weimar Republic to which it gave birth, and the rise of the Third Reich which it spawned. For it left the old Social Democratic movement irreversibly split, deprived the remaining rump of the SPD of all chances of future left-wing alliances and forced it into the position of a perpetual minority; and in the *Freikorps*, the volunteer battalions who waged and won the war for the Social Democrat Government, it gave birth to the frame of mind and attitudes of the future SA and SS, which were often their direct successors. The civil war of 1919 is thus a pivotal event in German twentieth-century history. But strangely enough it has almost completely vanished from the canvas of German history, erased and repressed. There are reasons for this.

One of them is shame. All the participants are ashamed of the part they played in the civil war. The defeated revolutionaries are ashamed of having nothing glorious to point to, no partial victory, not even a grandiose twilight, merely disorganized confusion, indecision, failure and defeat – and anonymous suffering and dying for thousands. But the victors, too, are ashamed. They formed a strange coalition: a coalition of Social Democrats and – Nazis. And both parties in this unnatural coalition were later reluctant to confess to what they had done: the Social Democrats that they had recruited the predecessors and prototypes of what were later to become the SA and the SS, and had unleashed these future Nazis on their own people; the Nazis that they had taken service under the Social Democrats and had been blooded under the Social Democrat aegis. History readily buries in silence what all participants remember with shame.

But there is another reason why the civil war of 1919 has disappeared from German memory and German historiography: it does not make a good 'yarn', no material for a spell-binding narrative – no drama with tension and memorable climaxes, no coherent action, no breath-taking battle between well-matched opponents. The bloody phenomenon rolled sluggishly across Germany without ever affecting the whole country at once. The slow fire always broke out somewhere when it had just been stamped out somewhere else. It began early in February on the North Sea coast, with Bremen as its centre; then, in the middle of February, the main theatre of war was suddenly in the Ruhr area, by the end of February in Thuringia and central Germany, at the beginning and in the middle of March in Berlin, in April in Bavaria, in May in Saxony; in between there were major episodes like the battles for Brunswick and Magdeburg, and innumerable smaller ones now known only to local historians: a bewildering, unstructured success of unconnected major and minor skirmishes, battles and massacres.

In each case the outcome was clear from the outset, and everything always followed the same pattern, in a constant, monotonous repetition. One can no more describe in detail the five or six months of civil war in 1919 than one can do it for their counterpart, the five or six days of revolution in November 1918. Just as then the same pattern had been repeated, with minor local deviations, throughout Germany, so it was again now: then the unresisted victory of the Revolution, now the triumphal march, not unresisted but irresistible, of the counter-Revolution. But there were differences; what had then been consummated with lightning speed, now proceeded with tortuous, methodical slowness; then little blood had been spilt, now it poured in rivers; then the Revolution had been the spontaneous act of the leaderless masses by which the Social Democrat leaders had most reluctantly allowed themselves to be raised to power, now the Counter-Revolution was a systematic military action ordered by these same Social Democrat leaders.

Of this there can be no doubt: the initiative for the civil war, the decision to fight it and therefore also – if we want to apply such concepts – the 'blame' for the civil war rested unquestionably with the Social Democrat leadership, especially with Ebert and Noske. At the most, the other side occasionally provided them with pretexts for an attack, sometimes not even that. After January in Berlin there was only one more 'second wave' of the Revolution, in Munich in April. Apart from this, Ebert and Noske were on the offensive from the start to the finish. To understand what happened one must above all try to put oneself in their place.

This need not take long as far as Noske is concerned. Noske was a simple man and a violent one, whose politics followed a primitive friend-foe pattern and who employed the primitive man's method of hitting out at everyone whom he considered his enemy at all times and with all available means. His later writings as much as his actions show him as incapable of the subtler distinctions, a man in love with violence, who by his whole mentality would have fitted into the Nazi party, the NSDAP, better than into the SPD. But Noske was not the 'head' of the civil war. He was merely Ebert's right hand – or rather his right fist. Ebert holds the key.

Ebert was no Nazi, not even unconsciously, and he was capable of making distinctions. He regarded himself throughout as a Social Democrat and after his own fashion as the friend of the workers. His aims were the aims of the pre-war SPD as he had found them: parliamentary government and social reform. But he was no revolutionary. For him revolution was both 'superfluous' (his favourite word) and lawless. He hated it 'like sin'. All he really wanted, and had ever wanted, had in fact been achieved in October 1918 when the Kaiser granted increased power to Parliament and the entry of the Social Democrats into the Government. All that was further gained by the November revolution he saw as foolishness, misunderstanding and mischief. The fact that he had been forced to pay lip-service to the Revolution only made him dislike it the more.

Ebert never had a bad conscience *vis-à-vis* the Revolution for having betrayed it; rather he was furious with it for forcing him to play a two-faced game for a time. If he did have a bad conscience, it was *vis-à-vis* the old order, for having had to act the revolutionary. Circumstances alone had compelled him to dissemble. He had had to ally himself to the Independents, to owe his position to the councils, to play the 'People's Commissar'; sad enough, but in his own eyes all null and void. At heart he had throughout remained the guardian of the old Reich and the old Reichstag majority.

When this majority was re-established by the elections for the National Assembly on January 19, 1919 (SPD 38 per cent, Centre Party 19 per cent, German Democratic Party 18 per cent), Ebert once again felt firm ground under his feet. For him this election cancelled out everything that had happened between November 9 and January 19. All the revolutionary institutions formed during those days, in particular the workers' and soldiers' councils, had in his view now lost their right to exist, and he quite failed to understand why they did not share this point of view. But naturally they did not share it, and that was why, regrettably, they had to be removed by force. This attitude of Ebert's, held in all good faith but extraordinarily subjective for all that, was at the root of the German civil war.

An almost grotesque event will illustrate how deep-seated this attitude was in Ebert. The Central Council of the Workers' and Soldiers' Councils, elected in Berlin by the National Congress of Councils, was nominally the highest revolutionary organ of state, from which the government of the 'People's Commissars' derived its authority. This Central Council was tame and meek beyond description. Composed exclusively of SPD members, it had never offered Ebert the slightest opposition, had even actively helped him in excluding Independents from the Government and was now quite prepared to transfer its powers to the National Assembly. But Ebert would not allow it to do even that: the Council had nothing left to transfer, he declared, now that the National Assembly was in being, all that was left for the Central Council to do was to shut up, pack up and disappear. This led to the first and only serious row between Ebert and the Central Council, which still went on leading an impotent shadow existence for a while. A grotesque episode without political significance, but it throws light on Ebert's political standpoint. The election of the National Assembly – which in turn promptly elected him provisional Reich President – had in his eyes created a new legality which latched on to the old one of October 1918. All that belonged to the interim period had now lost its status, retroactively. The Revolution was annulled *de jure*. It would now kindly annul itself *de facto*. The Workers' and Soldiers' Councils would have to go. Ebert, quite sincerely, regarded this as a matter of course.

But exist they did and obviously they took a very different view. For them the revolution had been annulled neither in law nor in fact, for them it remained the only source of any new legality. Even the tame Central Council argued: 'We can dismiss the People's Commissars, but not they us,' and the local Councils, still wielding local power everywhere, were at first inclined to greet Ebert's suggestions with bitter laughter. They knew they still had the backing of the working masses. These working masses consisted largely of demobilized soldiers fresh from the War, and almost everyone still had a gun at home. There was no shortage of arms and ammunition in Germany so soon after the War. Who would dare to send the people, victorious and armed, packing like a gang of schoolboys after a silly prank? As the chairman of the Leipzig workers' council, Kurt Geyer, was later to write sadly and self-critically, 'the possession of local power left the radical masses totally unable to see the true distribution of power in the overall structure'.

But not only the 'radical masses', the very councils, including their moderate SPD members, simply failed to understand why the Revolution should suddenly be treated as if it had not happened. Of course there was now a National Assembly; the National Congress of Councils had itself voted to elect one. But the Congress had never for a moment intended this as a step to abolish the Revolution. In the eyes of the councils the National Assembly in fact owed its own existence and legality to the resolution of the National Congress of Councils. It had quite clearly defined tasks: to draft a constitution and laws, to fix the budget, to control the Government. It was not meant to be omnipotent, and certainly not meant to annul the Revolution. Alongside it, the Councils went on regarding themselves as legitimate organs of state created by the Revolution, which would go on working by the side of the National Assembly as the provincial and communal authorities had previously worked alongside the imperial Reichstag. Just as until November 1918 there had been an elected Parliament in a state which, apart from this, was a class state, so it should be now – with the difference that the Revolution had replaced the rich and the aristocracy as the ruling class by workers and the other ranks. That was the view of the councils. The Soldiers' Councils still laid claim to disciplinary authority in the Army, the Workers' Councils still felt themselves to be the effective centre of local authority – by the right of revolution. If this was disputed, the whole issue became a question of power.

Noske stated this most unequivocally on January 21, during a Cabinet meeting: 'We must create a power factor to give the Government authority. In the course of a week an armed body of 22,000 men has been created. As a result relations with the Soldiers' Councils have shifted into a somewhat different key. Previously the Soldiers' Councils were the power factor; now we have become this power factor.' On the same day, faced with emissaries from the Soldiers' Council of the Seventh Army Corps protesting against the reintroduction of insignia of rank and the recruiting for the volunteer *Freikorps*, Noske threatened: 'You do not seem to have a clear idea of the powers of your Soldiers' Council; that is something we shall teach you in the next few days. There is going to be a big change! The Government is not going to put up with your measures and is going to intervene as it has already intervened elsewhere.' This last remark may have been an allusion to the events in Berlin in January and the murders of Liebknecht and Rosa Luxemburg.

Indeed, the Government 'intervened' at once – first in Bremen, then in the Ruhr, then in Thuringia and so on, step by step. By early February the civil war slowly moved into gear throughout the country. The occasions for intervention varied. Usually they were of a purely military nature – interference with the recruiting for the *Freikorps*, the refusal of Soldiers' Councils to reintroduce insignia of rank and the duty to salute (basing themselves on a resolution by the National Congress of Councils which Ebert and Noske had effectively set aside as early as January 19) sometimes they were strikes or local disorders.

In fact, there was, everywhere, only one real issue: the existence of the Workers' and Soldiers' Councils and, by extension, the legitimacy of the revolution. Noske's 'conqueror of cities', General Maercker, in command of the *Landesjägerkorps*, made this point quite openly:

The fight of the Reich government against the left-wing radicals was exclusively concerned with the maintenance of political power. The soldiers were sent into action with this purely political aim: as an element of force in the strengthening of internal politics. But the Government's weakness did not permit it to say so openly. It was afraid to show its hand and to announce that the volunteer force was being used to abolish Council rule wherever this was still to be found. For, in the last resort, that was what it was about. They got round this by using military matters as an excuse for intervention. This dishonest proceeding was not at all to my taste. I would have confronted the workers' leaders with more confidence if I could have told them openly: 'My presence means war on the council rule you are aiming at and on the despotism of the armed proletariat.'

Though Maercker was an arch-conservative, not to say reactionary, officer, he was an officer of the old school, accustomed to discipline and obedience, and his *Landesjägerkorps* was, at least during the 1919 civil war, a reasonably well-behaved and reliable government unit. One cannot say as much for most of the other *Freikorps*, recruited in a hectic rush during the months of civil conflict. In the end there were sixty-eight recognized *Freikorps* comprising, according to Noske, almost 400,000 men, each corps having sworn loyalty to its leader 'much as it must have been in Wallenstein's time' (Noske). The strangest thing is that Ebert and Noske put up with this and saw in it no cause for concern. Even more astonishing than the utter ruthlessness of their treatment of the left-wing revolutionaries to whom, after all, they owed their power, is the unsuspecting unconcern with which they armed their sworn enemies of the Right and taught them the taste of blood.

For right from the start there could not be the least doubt about the political attitudes of the overwhelming majority of these *Freikorps* leaders and their men. 'It would be a mild misrepresentation,' wrote von Oertzen, then a lieutenant in the *Garde-Kavallerie-Schützendivision*, 'to claim that the men in the then Government were to the liking of the officers in the Eden Hotel.' Indeed it would be. Colonel Reinhard, for example, later to become commander of this division and known to some as the 'liberator', to others as the 'butcher' of Berlin, spoke as early as Christmas 1918 of a 'Social Democrat witches' cauldron' and in a later address to his troops referred to the Government they served as 'riff-raff'. The leader of the *Eiserne Schar* (Iron Host), a Captain Gengler, wrote in his diary on January 21, 1919 of the Ebert Government: 'The day will come when I shall get my own back on this government and unmask the whole pitiful, miserable pack.' Lieutenant-Colonel Heinz, another well-known *Freikorps* leader, said a few months later: 'This state, born of revolt, will always be our enemy, never mind what sort of constitution it endows itself with and who is at its head . . . For the Reich! For the people! Fight against the Government! Death to the Democratic Republic!' And Herr von Heydebreck, then leader of the *Freikorps* 'Werwolf' (later a high-ranking SA leader and finally, together with his chief Röhm, shot by Hitler on June 30, 1934), said: 'War against the state of Weimar and Versailles! War every day and with all means! As I love Germany, so I hate the Republic of November 9!'

These were the attitudes of the leaders of those 400,000 men whom Ebert and Noske were now arming and unleashing against the workers, and to whom they entrusted the protection of the bourgeois republic they were bent on setting up as well as their own lives. In the case of Noske, who basically had much in common with them and who during the next year occasionally flirted with the idea of letting them make him a dictator, this can still be understood. In the case of Ebert it reveals a strange trait of blinkered incomprehension. Ebert, after all, was not dreaming of any SS state, but of a bourgeois Parliamentary democracy, joint government by the Social Democrats and the bourgeois centre, law, order and decency, a middle-class state with good conditions for the workers too. And to realize this dream, he now unleashed a pack which displayed almost all the characteristics of the future SA and SS, men of whom several were later to play a personal part in Hitler's seizure of power; in addition to Heydebreck, the German civil war produced names like Seldte and von Epp – the former to become a Minister in Hitler's Government, the latter Hitler's Governor of Bavaria.

Ebert was evidently quite blind as to the true nature of these early Nazis. On his political Right all he saw were friendly, cultured, well-meaning people and his only ambition had always been to have himself and his Party recognized by them as their equals and as capable of sharing in the Government. And had not this ambition been realized in October 1918? Had not Ludendorff himself finally granted, indeed ordered, even if unfortunately at the moment of defeat, the participation of the Social Democrats in the Government, for which Ebert had worked throughout the entire War? That this might have been a trap occurred to Ebert as little as did the insight that the Revolution, which in November provided the October Government with firm backing, had been his only chance of escape from that trap. All he could see was the honourable task of coming to the aid of the bourgeois state in its hour of need; he had remained at heart faithful to this task and expected nothing but gratitude from the Right. The only right-wing enemies he could envisage would have been monarchists (to his regret he had been unable to save the Monarchy), and the men in the *Freikorps* were certainly no monarchists. What they dreamed of and hoped for, what they fought and also murdered for, was something other than the Monarchy – something which would one day be put into words by a man who in those days was active as an obscure liaison man in the Bavarian Army in Munich. It was his spirit, as yet unrevealed, the spirit of the future concentration camps and extermination squads, which already in 1919 dominated the troops of the counter-Revolution which Ebert had summoned up and Noske was commanding. The Revolution of 1918 had been good-natured; the counter-Revolution was cruel. One could say in its defence that it had to fight, something the Revolution was spared, and that the other side, too, committed occasional atrocities and acts of brutality. But two facts tilt the scales: almost without exception the competently led and well-armed Government forces were vastly superior to the levies which were hastily assembled by the local councils and equipped only with small arms, with the result that casualties were very unevenly divided even during the actual fighting. And almost always the real terror – the summary courts, the arbitrary mass executions, the beatings and torturings – only started when the fighting was over, when the Government troops had been victorious, when they had nothing left to fear and could really let themselves go. In many German cities, horrors were committed during those days of which no history book tells.

Of course, the counter-Revolution was not dreaded by all; many saw it as a liberation and deliverance. While fear and sullen rage stalked the workers' districts in the conquered cities, while the street fighting left the streets deserted and unaccompanied officers venturing too far into the occupied areas risked being attacked and lynched, gratitude and rejoicing greeted the 'liberators' in the middle-class areas: beer, chocolates and packets of cigarettes, girls blowing kisses, children waving little flags. The civil war was a class war like all civil wars. Strange only that it was a Social Democrat government waging war against the working class.

Like any civil war, this one too saw an escalation of horrors as it developed. At the outset, in Bremen and central Germany, things had still been fairly moderate; in the Ruhr area, where sporadic fighting went on for weeks after the main clash in February, there were already many gruesome episodes. And dreadful things happened in Berlin, where in March, Noske's troops, commanded by Colonel Reinhard, moved in with a double aim: to occupy those workers' districts in the North and East of the city which had been left untouched in January, and to disarm the unreliable Berlin garrison troops which had taken part in the November Revolution, particularly the People's Naval Division

6

which was still in existence. One horrifying incident from this particular chapter has turned up in all the history books: when sailors of the People's Naval Division arrived unarmed in an office building in the Französische Strasse where they had been summoned to receive their demobilization papers and final pay (somehow the People's Naval Division was always concerned with its pay), thirty of them were grabbed without reason or warning, led into the courtyard, lined up against the wall and shot.

These thirty sailors were only a fraction of those massacred in Berlin in March. Noske was surely not exaggerating when he estimated the number at 'around twelve hundred'. He himself had issued the terrible order: 'Any person found offering armed resistance to Government troops is to be shot at once.' Colonel Reinhard further elaborated this order to shoot: 'In addition, all the inhabitants of houses from which troops are fired at, are to be brought out into the streets, irrespective of whether they affirm their innocence or not, and the houses are to be searched in their absence for arms; where arms are actually found, suspicious persons are to be shot.' In reading this one must have a mental picture of the overcrowded tenements of the East of Berlin. There are reports of what happened, as a result of this order, on March 11, 12 and 13, 1919, in the streets around the Alexanderplatz and in Berlin–Lichtenberg over which it is best to draw a veil.

These March battles in Berlin already saw instances of despair leading to hopeless resistance, of a violence hitherto unknown in the German civil war. But these March battles were not the climax of this bloody strife. The climax was reached a month later, in Munich.

13. The Munich Republic of Councils

In Bavaria the Revolution, from the beginning, took a different course from that in the rest of Germany.

Unlike the pattern of events in Berlin, the Revolution did not immediately fall into the hands of its enemies. Unlike elsewhere in the Reich it was not the work of leaderless masses. It had leadership and a leader, Kurt Eisner – a man who, unsupported by any organization, was in masterly control of the situation in his state for three months thanks to a unique mixture of inventiveness and energy, idealism and cunning adaptability, a sensitive nose and a firm grip.

As long as Kurt Eisner was alive, the Revolution in Bavaria was both successful and bloodless. His murder evoked an unparalleled public outcry and thirst for revenge, unequalled even by the reaction to the murder of Liebknecht and Rosa Luxemburg and it led to chaos. His death showed that Eisner had won the hearts of the ordinary people of Munich.

That was perhaps his most remarkable achievement, for he was in effect quite unqualified for the part of a Bavarian popular hero. He was no Bavarian, but a Berliner through and through; he was also a Jew and a man of letters – a picture-book intellectual with beard and spectacles, and a bit of a Bohemian. Eisner had passed his Berlin childhood between the Opernplatz and the Kastanienwäldchen; his father had a shop in Unter den Linden selling military accessories and decorations, and held the royal warrant. His prodigal son turned into an aesthete and a Socialist; but became a journalist rather than a politician, scoring his chief successes as a drama critic. In 1907, at the age of forty, chance took him to Munich. In the SPD, where he was not particularly prominent, he, if anything, belonged to the right-wing, liberal, semi-bourgeois section. Only the War drove him further to the

An die Bevölkerung Münchens!

Das furchtbare Schicksal, das über das deutsche Volk hereingebrochen, hat zu einer elementaren Bewegung der Münchner Arbeiter und Soldaten geführt. Ein provisorischer Arbeiter-, Soldaten- und Bauernrat hat sich in der Nacht zum 8. November im Landtag konstituiert.

Bayern ist fortan ein Freistaat.

Eine Volksregierung, die von dem Vertrauen der Massen getragen wird, soll unverzüglich eingesetzt werden.

Eine konstituierende Nationalversammlung, zu der alle mündigen Männer und Frauen das Wahlrecht haben, wird so schnell wie möglich einberufen werden.

Eine neue Zeit hebt an!

Bayern will Deutschland für den Völkerbund rüsten.

Die demokratische und soziale Republik Bayern hat die moralische Kraft, für Deutschland einen Frieden zu erwirken, der es vor dem Schlimmsten bewahrt. Die jetzige Umwälzung war notwendig, um im letzten Augenblick durch die Selbstregierung des Volkes die Entwicklung der Zustände ohne allzuschwere Erschütterung zu ermöglichen, bevor die feindlichen Heere die Grenzen überfluten oder nach dem Waffenstillstand die demobilisierten deutschen Truppen das Chaos herbeiführen.

Der Arbeiter-, Soldaten- und Bauernrat wird strengste Ordnung sichern. Ausschreitungen werden rücksichtslos unterdrückt. Die Sicherheit der Person und des Eigentums wird verbürgt.

Die Soldaten in den Kasernen werden durch Soldatenräte sich selbst regieren und Diszplin aufrecht erhalten. Offiziere, die sich den Forderungen der veränderten Zeit nicht widersetzen, sollen unangetastet ihren Dienst versehen.

Wir rechnen auf die schaffende Mithilfe der gesamten Bevölkerung. Jeder Arbeiter an der neuen Freiheit ist willkommen! Alle Beamte bleiben in ihren Stellungen. Grundlegende soziale und politische Reformen werden unverzüglich ins Werk gesetzt.

Die Bauern verbürgen sich für die Versorgung der Städte mit Lebensmitteln. Der alte Gegensatz zwischen Land und Stadt wird verschwinden. Der Austausch der Lebensmittel wird rationell organisiert werden.

Arbeiter, Bürger Münchens! Vertraut dem Großen und Gewaltigen, das in diesen schicksalschweren Tagen sich vorbereitet!

Helft alle mit, daß sich die unvermeidliche Umwandlung rasch, leicht und friedlich vollzieht.

In dieser Zeit des sinnlos wilden Mordens verabscheuen wir alles Blutvergießen. Jedes Menschenleben soll heilig sein.

Bewahrt die Ruhe und wirkt mit an dem Aufbau der neuen Welt!

Der Bruderkrieg der Sozialisten ist für Bayern beendet. Auf der revolutionären Grundlage, die jetzt gegeben ist, werden die Arbeitermassen zur Einheit zurückgeführt.

Es lebe die bayerische Republik!

Es lebe der Frieden!

Es lebe die schaffende Arbeit aller Werktätigen!

München, Landtag, in der Nacht zum 8. November 1918.

Der Rat der Arbeiter, Soldaten und Bauern:

Der erste Vorsitzende: Kurt Eisner.

Bekanntmachung. Zur Aufrechterhaltung der Ordnung und Sicherheit arbeitet von heute an das gesamte Polizei- und Sicherheitspersonal im Auftrag und unter Kontrolle des Arbeiter- und Soldatenrates.

Den Anordnungen dieser Organe ist unbedingt Folge zu leisten.

Erklärung des Münchner Polizeipräsidenten.

Ich verpflichte mich, bei der Ausübung des Sicherheitsdienstes den Anordnungen des Arbeiter- und Soldatenrates München Folge zu leisten. Sofern ich dieser Verpflichtung nicht nachkommen kann, muß ich mir das Recht des Rücktrittes vorbehalten.

München, 8. November 1918, morgens 1 Uhr.

K. Polizeipräsident: gez. v. Beck.

Kurt Eisner's proclamation of the revolutionary republic of Bavaria.

left and into the USPD which had little significance in Bavaria as an organized Party. Moreover, Eisner did nothing to build up the Party. He was no party politician, no party leader. But in January 1918 he was active as a strike organizer – his first venture into the political limelight. He was arrested and held for nine months without a hearing. In October he was released. In November he made the Munich Revolution.

Incredible though it sounds, he made the Revolution. The November Revolution in Munich was a one-man show. All those events which in Berlin, during the weekend of November 9 and 10, had constituted the Revolution – getting the soldiers to change their minds, the mass marches, the proclamation of the Republic, the Revolutionary Parliament, the formation of a Government, the election of the Councils – had happened two days earlier in Munich, in a somewhat different order, during the night of November 7 to 8, under the direction of Kurt Eisner, and with Kurt Eisner in all the leading roles. He was at the same time the Otto Wels and the Liebknecht, the Emil Barth and the Scheidemann, in a certain sense even the Ebert of the Munich Revolution, inasmuch as he was the only one to know exactly what he wanted and how to bring it about.

The Munich Revolution began on the afternoon of Thursday, November 7, with a mass meeting on the Theresienwiese. The Bavarian Royal Government had permitted this demonstration organized by the SPD in order to provide a safety valve to allow the revolutionary mood to let off steam. The SPD leader, Erhard Auer, had given reassuring undertakings: he had firm control of his people and nothing untoward would happen. This Eisner would be 'pushed against the wall'. In fact, after speeches demanding the abolition of the Monarchy and the overthrow of the Government, Auer marched off with a section of the demonstrators in a neat procession through the city centre to the Friedensengel where everybody dispersed. But Eisner had meanwhile led an equally large column in the opposite direction – into the North of Munich, towards the barracks.

There, in the early evening, the decisive act of any *coup d'état* was staged – the 'reversal' of armed power. Then, still under

Eisner's personal direction, the first Workers' and Soldiers' Councils were constituted in the Matthäserbräu; then, late in the night (the King had already left Munich and armed soldiers were driving through the city centre in trucks and taking up sentry positions outside public buildings) the first meeting of these Councils (the 'Revolutionary Parliament'), held in the Prannerstrasse building of the Provincial Assembly, proclaimed the Republic and nominated Eisner as Prime Minister.

The next morning Eisner held decisive political discussions: with the Royal Prime Minister, who surrendered his office under protest, and with Auer, the SPD leader, who – swallowing his rage – was persuaded to take over Home Affairs under Eisner. In the afternoon Eisner presented his Cabinet at the first plenary session of the 'Provisional National Council'. The Munich Revolution was complete, accomplished in one breathless solo run within twenty-four hours. No shot had been fired, no blood had been spilt. And the man who had performed this trick, a mere nonentity the day before, now held all the strings.

That evening Eisner spoke before the Provisional National Council. 'For a man who had had little sleep for twenty-four hours his brief speech was surprisingly literary' – to quote the American historian of the Bavarian Revolution, Allan Mitchell, whose attitude to Eisner is highly critical, perhaps even a little jaundiced.

Eisner's speech of November 8 was not only literary, it was statesmanlike. 'In times of more tranquil development' a National Assembly would be called together to draft the final form of the Republic; until then the people would have to govern directly through the 'elemental impetus' of the Revolutionary Councils. What was now essential, if a bearable Peace were to be achieved, was a clearly visible new start, a complete severance from the old state and, above all, total abandonment of its War policy. 'A Government which has assumed all the responsibilities of the past faces a terrible Peace' Eisner said, with a clear allusion to Berlin.

Eisner, as opposed to Ebert, saw the international position of the vanquished Germany very clearly from the start and had a clear idea of foreign policy. He saw the dangers of a dictated peace and tried to anticipate them by providing impressive proof of a clear breach with the past at home and by establishing direct contacts abroad, with the Western powers, especially with America; he had no liking of Bolshevist Russia. This policy of Eisner's later fell on deaf ears in Berlin; there, particularly in matters of foreign policy, much importance was attached to unbroken continuity with the *Kaiserreich*. Eisner's ruthless break with the War policy of 1914 was regarded as 'dirtying one's own nest' – and subsequently there was speechless surprise when the victors in Versailles treated Ebert's 'new' Germany simply as the vanquished *Kaiserreich*.

But what is of interest here is not Eisner's foreign policy so much as his management of the Bavarian Revolution, which deserves the epithet 'masterly' – even if it remains an open question whether a successful revolution in Bavaria could in the long run have stood up to a successful counter-Revolution in the rest of Germany. Eisner was the only man in Germany who had enough shrewd insight to grasp what the German Revolution was aiming at and ably to assist its birth, in contrast to Ebert, whose only thought was to throttle the Revolution – in contrast also to Liebknecht who demanded of it what it never intended. Ebert's true adversary was not Liebknecht, it was Eisner. Not without reason Arthur Rosenberg in his *History* has called him the only creative statesman of the German Revolution.

What did the revolutionary masses in Germany want? Not – at least not immediately – Socialism. Nowhere in November were factories occupied; demands for socialization came into play much later, and effectively only in the case of the miners. The first and predominant aim was an end to the War and the overthrow of Military Government, together with the overthrow of the Monarchy. But the overthrow of Military Government and of the Monarchy had more far-reaching implications: namely the overthrow of the ruling classes. The Workers' and Soldiers' Councils, which were both the creation and the essence of the Revolution, wanted to become the successors to the old officers' corps and the old bureaucracy. The state was in future to recruit its upper echelons from a new ruling class, not from the aristocracy and the Grande Bourgeoisie, but from the other ranks and the working class. The new state was to be a workers' state; Eisner went further: it was also to be a peasants' state. Bavaria under Eisner was the only German state where Peasants' Councils played an important part from the start.

Did this mean dictatorship by the Councils? By no means. The Councils themselves had in fact decreed the election of a National Assembly, and Eisner himself arranged for the election of a Bavarian Diet, even if he would have liked to delay it and was in no hurry to summon it after its election. The councils were far from wanting dictatorial powers. Neither council dictatorship nor parliamentary dictatorship were in their minds, but a constitutional councils' democracy; basically a constitutional structure much like the familiar Bismarckian one, but upside down – or rather downside up. The Workers' and Soldiers' Councils as the pillars of state, replacing the aristocracy and Grande Bourgeoisie; a reunited Social Democratic Party as the governing party and a permanent government independent of Parliament as the conservatives had been. And side by side with this a Parliament freely elected by the entire people, including the – no longer – ruling classes, to act as a representative, legislative and controlling organ, perhaps with even greater powers than the old Reichstag had enjoyed, but without omnipotence. That was the constitution for which the revolutionaries all over Germany struggled. Anyone who – like Eisner – had ears to hear could make this out quite clearly from all its manifestations, in words and deeds.

Both Ebert and Liebknecht were deaf to this. Both – though with diametrically opposite hopes – could only see a simple choice: dictatorship by the Councils (*Rätediktatur*) or a bourgeois Parliamentary democracy. Eisner was alone in seeing that the Revolution was in fact not posing this alternative at all. This bohemian man of letters was, in 1918, Germany's only revolutionary realist. He realized that the true choice lay not between rule by the Councils or by Parliament, but between Revolution and counter-Revolution; and that Revolution implied neither dictatorship by the Councils nor dictatorship by a Parliament, but a system of checks and balances between the power of the

Councils and the powers of a Parliament. He also realized that the new councillors were inexperienced and needed time to warm up. This is why he would have liked to delay the elections to the Provincial Assembly and why, when he failed in this, he at least put off its meeting as long as possible.

As was to have been expected in Catholic Bavaria, the elections had resulted in a bourgeois-Catholic majority. The Bavarian Popular Party – the same party which nowadays calls itself the CSU – emerged as numerically the strongest, with 66 of the 180 representatives. The SPD came second with 61. The USPD, to which Eisner belonged but to which he had never paid much serious attention, remained a tiny minority – with no more than three of the 180 seats in the Provincial Assembly.

Eisner was unperturbed. His mind was focused on revolutionary, not on parliamentary politics. The bourgeoisie might indeed provide the majority of electors, but the War and the way it had ended had left it discredited, intimidated, passive – whereas the masses of the workers and soldiers, whether they voted SPD or USPD, were in a state of high revolutionary fervour and potency. Their revolutionary organ was the Councils, not the parties. And Eisner knew he had the backing of these masses in insisting on retaining the Councils and limiting the power of Parliament. This led to conflict between Eisner and his Home Secretary, the SPD leader, Auer, and to a crisis between the Councils and the Provincial Assembly.

This crisis took visible shape in the week before the Provincial Assembly's first meeting on February 21: the Parliamentary Parties held meetings in one wing of the Assembly building, the Councils were in session in the other. The Parliamentary Parties, under Auer's guidance, were labouring to put together a coalition Government of Social Democrats and Liberals which would have kept the strongest party in Parliament, the Bavarian Popular Party (BVP), in opposition. The Councils were getting ready for a 'second revolution' in the event that Parliament should try to abolish them as had been done elsewhere in Germany. Eisner was ready to resign as Prime Minister and to yield the Parliamentary arena, for the time being, to Auer; but he was determined to remain at the head of the Councils and, if need be, to lead the 'second revolution'. His demand was for the Councils to be 'anchored' in the new Constitution.

A trial of strength appeared imminent. Its outcome was open. There were no *Freikorps* in Bavaria, and those parts of the armed forces which were not yet demobilized were overwhelmingly controlled by their Soldiers' Councils. But there was also still the chance of a compromise; Bavaria had until now been an example to the German Revolution; in spite of some tense moments no blood had been shed. Often with great personal courage and always with great skill, Eisner had contrived to conciliate in dangerous situations. Perhaps this time, too, he might have succeeded in achieving the balance between Council power and Parliamentary control which was his object.

But when, on the morning of February 21, 1919, a few minutes before ten, he turned the corner from the Promenadenplatz into the Prannerstrasse, in order to attend the opening meeting of the Provincial Assembly, his resignation speech in his attaché case, he was murdered.

The murderer – a young man in a raincoat who stepped from a house doorway towards Eisner and, at close range, fired two revolver bullets into his head – was a half-Jewish Nazi. Count Arco-Valley had been expelled from the *Thule* Club – an association which later justly boasted that it had been the original nucleus of the Nazi movement – because he had kept quiet about his Jewish mother. This is why, as the founder of the *Thule* Club, Rudolf von Sebottendorff, was later to write that Arco-Valley wanted 'to prove that even a half-Jew was capable of an heroic deed'.

Eisner died immediately. His murderer was shot at and seriously injured by one of Eisner's bodyguards, but he later recovered, was sentenced, pardoned and lived until 1945.

News of the atrocity spread at once throughout Munich, arousing horror and anger. It was followed by a second one within the hour. A butcher's assistant called Lindner had no sooner heard of Eisner's murder than he grabbed his pistol in frenzied rage, rushed to the Provincial Assembly building, forced his way in, levelled his gun at the SPD leader, Auer, who was just voicing conventional outrage in a memorial speech in honour of his murdered opposite number, and shot him down. It is interesting that Lindner evidently took it for granted that the murder of a revolutionary leader would have been instigated by whoever was leader of the SPD at the time, an assumption indicative of the state of things in Germany at the time. In fact Auer was quite innocent of the murder. He survived his injuries but for years was politically inactive.

This hour was to have immeasurable consequences. The two dominant minds in Bavarian politics were suddenly gone. In their place there was everywhere a sudden wild upsurge of emotion. The whole city, indeed the whole country, at one fell stroke presented a picture of anarchy – everywhere armed men raging through the streets on foot, in cars or in trucks; shootings, random arrests, beatings and looting, panic, rage, and thirst for revenge.

The Provincial Assembly had scattered in a panic. There was no longer any Government: of the eight ministers constituting it, one was dead, one desperately injured, one in hiding, two had fled from the raging cauldron of Munich; only three tried to carry on with the routine work in their ministries, without Cabinet meetings and without contact. A general strike had been proclaimed, a state of siege declared. Thousands made the pilgrimage to the scene of the murder on the Promenadenplatz where around the huge bloodstain a sort of altar with a picture of Eisner had been erected on bayonets. Eisner's funeral, which took place a few days later with regal splendour, became a gigantic demonstration of enraged grief. Vast numbers of country people poured into the city to join it, and the Bavarian mountaineers with their chamois-tufts and leather shorts marched seriously and solemnly behind the coffin of this Berlin Jew who had, they felt, understood them so well. No one knew what was to happen next.

In all this chaos the Councils provided the only reasonably intact authority left. Their Central Council, under the chairmanship of the young elementary school teacher Ernst Niekisch, later to acquire fame as a writer and glory as a martyr of the Third Reich, endeavoured to implement 'Eisner's legacy' – i.e. to bring about a compromise between the Councils, the socialist parties, and the Provincial Assembly. There was no longer any mention of a bourgeois-socialist coalition Government. After weeks of confused negotiations, a new Socialist Government finally emerged under a man from the SPD, Johannes Hoffmann, which on March 17 was given comprehensive authority by a short session of the Provincial Assembly. In form it was a dictatorial Government; in fact it lacked the foundations of power. It did not wish to be regarded as a government of the councils, but apart from the Councils it had no backing. It did not command a majority in the Provincial Assembly, and in the last resort the Councils had little faith in it. The Hoffmann Government was in the long run unable to carry on. Since Eisner's murder and Auer's elimination, the weight of circumstances in Bavaria tended in the direction of a Republic of Councils, a *Räterepublik* – simply because the Councils had now become the only more or less substantial source of power, the only alternative to anarchy.

Two major problems remained: firstly, whether a Republic of Councils could come into – and remain – in being in Bavaria when everywhere else in Germany Noske's *Freikorps* were liquidating the Councils; secondly, whether the Councils were at all in a position to govern – particularly now that Eisner was dead.

In addition to the moderates like Niekisch striving to implement Eisner's legacy, there were now two new forces locked in battle in the Councils: on the one hand a body of intellectuals characterized by a mixture of high-mindedness, ambition and political ineptitude – expressionist poets like Erich Mühsam and Ernst Toller, academic theoreticians like the literary historian Gustav Landauer and the economists Otto Neurath and Silvio Gesell; on the other, for the first time in the history of the German Revolution, the Communists; more precisely *one* Communist, Eugen Leviné, a young man of startling and tempestuous energy, who, quite unlike Liebknecht or Rosa Luxemburg, was perhaps made of the stuff to become a German Lenin or Trotsky.

Leviné – born in Petersburg, the son of German-Jewish parents, raised in Germany – had as late as early March been sent to Munich by Party Headquarters in Berlin in order to get a

Bavarian Communist Party going. Of the seven men he had found constituting the Munich KPD, he had thrown out five and within one month had created a well-disciplined, if small, Party organization, and was now beginning to make himself felt in the Councils as a hard, domineering, cool-headed revolutionary. During this phase he was the bitterest opponent of a Bavarian Republic of Councils: in his view the Councils were not yet ripe for the task of government. They would first have to be firmly reorganized, disciplined, armed: only then would they be ready to seize power – but then complete power, without coalition partners and without concessions. All or nothing – no constitutional council democracy, but a dictatorship of the proletariat. When on April 5 the *Räterepublik* was in fact proclaimed, Leviné and his Communists were the only ones to vote against and to refuse to participate. One week later, on April 13, they nevertheless took over the *Räterepublik*, by a *coup d'état* within the *coup d'état*.

What had happened meanwhile? A civil war had broken out.

*

Curiously enough it had been the Minister for military affairs in Hoffmann's Social Democrat Government, a man called Schneppenhorst, who provided the final impetus for the proclamation of the *Räterepublik* on April 5. His motives have been much debated, but in the last analysis they are pretty evident: he wanted to confront the Councils with tangible evidence of their own inability to govern, in order then to abolish them as quickly and painlessly as possible, with the aid of a military *coup* by the Munich garrison over whom he had at least partial control. Both he and the Hoffmann Government, who had taken refuge in Bamberg, were anxious not only to be rid of the councils, but above all to do this under their own steam. They had no wish to open the country to the Prussian *Freikorps* whose services had been offered by Noske.

The military *coup* accordingly took place, as planned, on Palm Sunday, April 13 but it failed. In the course of a bloody five-hour street battle which began in the Marienplatz and ended with the storming of the main railway station, Schneppenhorst's troops were beaten by a hurriedly assembled 'red' force led by a sailor called Rudolf Eglhofer. They fled from Munich by train. A second attempt to take Munich – this time from the outside – by Bavarian troops loyal to the Government ended three days later in their defeat. In an encounter at Dachau on April 16, the 'red army' overcame its 'white' enemies and occupied Dachau. The 'red' commander in this encounter was the poet Ernst Toller.

But now the die was cast. The Hoffmann Government in Bamberg swallowed its pride and called upon Noske for help; 20,000 men from the *Freikorps* in Prussia and Württemberg, under the command of the Prussian, General van Oven, moved into Bavaria from the north and west.

Eugen Leviné had meanwhile taken over the Council administration in Munich. He abandoned all restraint and cast his political realism overboard; the situation was now critical, the time had come to fight, and he was not prepared to leave the fighting to the moderates around Niekisch, who were still inclined towards negotiation and compromise, nor to the starry-eyed, like Toller and Landauer.

What Leviné failed to see, or closed his eyes to in heroic self-deception, was that the time for fighting, like the time for negotiating, was already past. He did indeed succeed in getting together a 'red army' of about 10,000 men, under the command of the energetic Eglhofer, and to give them rudimentary organization and training. But that was not enough to pit against the superior forces relentlessly approaching, it was not enough even for any noticeable resistance.

The area of the Munich *Räterepublik* extended for all practical purposes no further than Dachau in the north, Garmisch and Rosenheim in the south. All food supplies were cut off; Munich was starving. At the same time there was a grotesque shortage of legal tender: the Munich branch of the *Reichsbank* had removed all its stocks of cash and all the printing plates for bank notes. Leviné ordered the confiscation of bank accounts and safe deposits, and requisitioned the private food hoards of middle-class households: desperate measures, taken in a rage and enraging others. He was also the first German revolutionary to arrest political opponents.

In the end, when the guns were blasting in the streets, eight of them, members of the *Thule* Club, were shot, together with two officers taken prisoners-of-war. Leviné was not responsible for this deed; it has never been established beyond doubt who was. It was the only act of true terror which can be blamed on the German Revolution – and it was to be terribly avenged.

In the meantime, the Council government had broken up: a majority, led by Toller, forced Leviné to resign on April 29, reproaching him with a policy of violence, while they made one more vain attempt to resume negotiations with Bamberg. The 'red army' remained and went on fighting on its own. But it could no longer save anything. On April 29 Dachau fell, on April 30 Noske's troops penetrated the Munich city area from three directions. On the afternoon of May 2 the last resistance collapsed.

And now a 'white terror' ensued such as no German city, not even Berlin in March, had yet experienced. For a whole week the conquerors were at liberty to shoot, and everyone 'suspected of Spartacism' – in effect Munich's entire working-class population – was outlawed. Josef Hofmiller, a right-wing senior teacher and literary critic, who kept a diary to record the events, noted as late as May 10 a statement by the publisher Bruckmann that 'the maid-servants in the entire house were in a state of excitement because people were being shot there every day'. He also tells, with much equanimity, of 'Spartacists' whom he saw being dragged out of wine-bars or railway trains and shot then and there. 'We have got quite used to the constant shooting.'

This 'white' terror displayed an unmistakable trait of sadism. For example, Gustav Landauer, the highly cultivated Minister of Education in the first Council government, was literally trampled to death in the courtyard of the Stadelheim prison – not in an access of fury, but in a sort of victorious frolic. His air of a Jewish scholar may have triggered something off in his torturers. Other scenes of horror, with a pronouncedly sexual flavour and often with women 'Spartacist wenches' as their victims are reported by Manfred von Killinger, then a *Freikorps* leader, with reminiscent relish in his book *Ernstes und Heiteres aus dem Putschleben*

('Memories Gay and Grim from the Time of the Coup'). Von Killinger was later to have a splendid career under Hitler.

May 1919 in Munich was also peculiar in that it had something about it of a foreign invasion and occupation. The Prussian *Freikorps* felt and behaved like victors in a conquered country; they thought the Munich proletarians unappealing, sluttish and dirty, looked down upon them and did not understand their dialect. Probably that was the cause of the misunderstanding which finally brought the random shootings to an end. On May 6 twenty-one members of a Catholic association of journeymen (*Gesellenverein*), who, feeling safe under the liberators, had ventured to hold a reunion, were raided by these very liberators and – as was now usual – shot without further ado. A meeting of young men evidently belonging to the working class had seemed an obvious 'Spartacist gathering', and when the terrified victims endeavoured to explain themselves, their Bavarian dialect may have contributed to their complete failure to make themselves understood.

After this embarrassing mishap the frenzied executions abated. Further 'tidying-up' was left to the courts and summary jurisdiction. The defeated got short shrift from them, too. It rained death sentences. Leviné used his court hearing to make a good exit. 'We Communists,' he said in his concluding address, 'are all dead men on leave. It is up to you to decide whether my pass is to be extended once more or whether I shall be drafted to join Karl Liebknecht and Rosa Luxemburg.' Two hours later he was shot. He died shouting: 'Long Live World Revolution.'

14. *Nemesis*

By the middle of 1919 the back of the German Revolution had been broken. The SPD was left governing a bourgeois state. The counter-Revolution it had summoned wielded the real power behind the scenes. Seen from the outside, the SPD had never before – or since – made such a splendid showing. In the Reich, in Prussia, in Bavaria it filled all the top positions. But its power was illusory. Within the bourgeois state which it had reconstituted, the SPD remained a foreign body. To the counter-revolutionary *Freikorps*, which had assisted in the reconstitution, it remained an enemy. This Party of the workers had destroyed the foundations of its own power when it had crushed the revolution of the working masses.

In fact, the SPD had throughout aimed at restoring the *status quo* of October 1918. Those had been the days when its modest aims had seemed accomplished. It had at last 'grown into' the State and the Government; and, more than that, had been courted and wooed by the administrative and social establishment. That unfortunate November Revolution had temporarily disturbed this idyll, but now that it was happily a thing of the past, the Social Democrat leaders thought their idyll restored – even though there was no Kaiser enthroned at the top. As in October 1918, the SPD was once again governing a Parliamentary state hand in hand with the Centre and the Progressives. The 'Weimar Coalition' was nothing other than the old Reichstag Majority – the same coalition which in October 1918 had carried the Government of Max von Baden.

And yet everything was different. In October 1918 the Revolution had been imminent; now it was over and done with. Then the bourgeoisie and the feudal class had been scared; now they had regained their self-confidence. Then they had needed the

SPD to shoulder the burden of the capitulation and to throttle the Revolution. Now that both these tasks were accomplished, the SPD was no longer needed except perhaps as a scapegoat and whipping boy for the defeat and the post-war misery. From the middle of 1919 onwards, to quote Ernst Troeltsch, the most perceptive of contemporary observers, 'a wave from the right' came sweeping over Germany. The Social Democrats became the 'November Criminals' and 'defeatist politicians' who had 'stabbed the German Army in the back'.

Even the relationship with their partners in the Government, the bourgeois centre parties, was no longer what it had been. Before October 1918, in the struggle for parliamentary government, the three parties had tugged at the same rope. Now Democrats and Centre Party were no longer the SPD's allies, but its watchdogs. They made sure that the Social Democrats did not in any way disturb the capitalist economy or the Catholic Church. Without an absolute majority in Parliament and without potential coalition partners on the Left, the Social Democrats were forced to rely on the parties of the bourgeois centre. But the centre parties had the choice, if they preferred, of governing in alliance with the parties of the bourgeois Right – who in turn had the choice of either forming a bourgeois block in Parliament or making common cause with open counter-Revolution. The counter-Revolution had become a force – in many eyes the only real force. Since August 1919 its organizational centre was to be found in the *Nationale Vereinigung* (National Union), a group of conspirators preparing a *coup d'état*. Its leaders were Wolfgang Kapp, from East Prussia, and Captain Pabst, who had organized the murder of Liebknecht and Luxemburg; behind them stood Ludendorff, who had meanwhile returned from Sweden.

Between November 1918 and summer 1919 Germany had faced the choice: revolution or counter-revolution? Now the choice was simply: bourgeois restoration or counter-revolution? (Ten years later the question was to be: Which kind of counter-revolution?)

The outcome of this choice depended as much on the soldiers as on the politicians. The 400,000-man *Reichswehr*, formed in March 1919 from the *Freikorps*, was a political army through and through, and an army of the Right at that. Like the political Right, the military Right had a cautious conservative element as well as more reckless characters who were impatient for action. The one group was prepared to give the bourgeois-parliamentary state a chance under a government of the bourgeois block; the other wanted a military *coup d'état* and dictatorship. Neither group had any use for the Social Democrats. At best some of them made a personal exception in the case of Noske.

In July 1919, after the signing of the Versailles Treaty, Hindenburg and Groener, the chiefs of the old High Command, had resigned. Since then politics had been almost as prominent in the *Reichswehr* as in the National Assembly. Almost every unit had its own political character, almost every general his own political ideas. Two men slowly emerged as the leading figures of the two political wings of the *Reichswehr*: Hans von Seeckt, chief of the General Staff, who was anxious – for the time being, at least – to 'de-politicize' the *Reichswehr*; and Walther von Lüttwitz, Commander-in-Chief of Group Command I, the 'Father of the *Freikorps*', who already by 1919 was constantly voicing political demands (e.g. prohibition of strikes, abolition of unemployment benefits). Since the summer of 1919 the *Reichswehr*'s plans for a dictatorship were a frequent subject of discussion. Noske was several times involved in such discussions, and played a somewhat questionable part in them. It is true that he turned down the idea of becoming dictator as the result of a military coup, but he took no steps against the officers who approached him with such a proposal, and there is no evidence that he informed his ministerial colleagues of his repeated flirtations with men planning high treason. If all these plans for military coups and dictatorships in the second half of 1919 came to nothing, it was chiefly because the would-be insurgents among the officers could not decide whom to make into a dictator. Someone from their own ranks? Noske? Kapp? Ludendorff? They lacked a convincing candidate: there was as yet no Hitler. When the year 1920 arrived, the never-ending talk of a coup had become commonplace and was no longer taken seriously. Yet that was the moment when the situation did become serious.

On January 10, 1920 the Treaty of Versailles took effect, limiting the German Army to 100,000 men; the Navy to 15,000. This meant a drastic reduction in the 1919 400,000-strong *Reichswehr*. Most of the *Freikorps* would have to be disbanded willy-nilly. In fact they were no longer required: they had not been recruited to defend the country but to overthrow the Revolution, and they had accomplished this task. Now they had become a potential source of disorder and a danger to State and Government.

But they were not prepared to be sent packing, nor were the political generals willing to part with the instrument of their political power. Rather than renounce it, they would put it to use. Hence the military *coup d'état* of March 13, 1920 which has gone down in history as the 'Kapp Putsch'.

The name is misleading – as misleading as the name 'Spartacus week' which has been attached to the week of revolution in Berlin in January 1919. Kapp and his 'National Union' played as lamentable a secondary part in the drama of these March days as the fifty-three-man Revolutionary Committee had done in the previous year's January tragedy. Then there had been spontaneous mass action, now there was military insurrection. It was led not by Kapp but by General von Lüttwitz and was occasioned by Noske's decree of February 29, 1920, ordering the disbanding of the *Marinebrigade Ehrhardt*.

The Ehrhardt Brigade, numbering 5,000 men, was a *Freikorps*, originally recruited from officers and NCOs of the Navy, later reinforced with men from the *Baltikum*, German troops who as late as 1919 had fought in Latvia against Bolshevist units. In the civil war the brigade had seen action in Berlin and Munich. Militarily speaking, it was an élite unit, politically it was extremely anti-Government. Its colours were black, white and red (the colours of the Imperial German flag as well as of the subsequent Nazi emblem) and its orders of the day habitually made mockery of the ministers. Since January 1920, when General von Lüttwitz had moved it to the Döberitz military camp near Berlin, the Brigade wore the Swastika on its steel helmets. As early as 1920 the spirit of this unit was unmistakably that of the future *Waffen-SS*. The brigade responded to the disbandment decree of February

29 with a big parade on the following day, to which the Reich Defence Minister was not invited. At this parade General von Lüttwitz declared: 'I shall not permit such an élite band of men to be torn asunder at so storm-laden a moment of time.' It was a public breach of obedience to the Government, and he meant what he said.

Some of his staff officers were frightened and during the next few days tried to stop and deflect Lüttwitz. As a first step they arranged a discussion between him and the leaders of the two Parliamentary right-wing parties. These had just initiated a political action of their own: they were demanding the dissolution of the National Assembly and new elections for the *Reichstag*, a cabinet of 'experts' and the immediate election by plebiscite of the Reich President – completely constitutional demands but ones which, now that the 'wave from the right' was on the move, they hoped would lead to the elimination of the SPD from the Government. The Government parties had of course rejected these demands but it was hoped to push them through with the help of a large-scale propaganda campaign in the ensuing weeks or months. They therefore had no use for a coup at this point in time. Lüttwitz took note of their demands, but was not to be dissuaded from his plans for a *coup d'état*. In contrast with the leaders of the right-wing parties he felt there was no time to spare. He did not want to risk the loss of his best unit. He felt himself to be under pressure.

This feeling grew stronger in the days that followed, for Noske now removed the Ehrhardt Brigade from Lüttwitz's command and placed it under that of the naval authorities, in the hope that these would implement his disbandment order. Lüttwitz ignored this instruction, but before he went too far his staff officers managed to persuade him to seek an interview with Ebert. Ebert was good-naturedly prepared to receive the mutinous general ('The old gentleman is eccentric, after all,' he said). On March 10 at 6 p.m., Lüttwitz, with a large entourage, called upon Ebert who, for his part, had co-opted Noske. The discussion was catastrophic. 'Sharply and with the utmost vehemence' Lüttwitz demanded new elections and 'expert ministers', as he had learned from the leaders of the right-wing parties, but in addition his own nomination as Commander-in-Chief of the entire *Reichswehr* and the retraction of the disbandment orders. Ebert and Noske rejected these demands, Ebert in a paternal manner, stating his reasons at length. Noske, irritated and curt, said he expected the General's resignation by the next morning. They parted in anger.

There was no resignation the next morning. Instead Lüttwitz went to see Hermann Ehrhardt in Döberitz and asked him whether he and his brigades could occupy Berlin that very evening. Ehrhardt had to say that he needed a day for preparations but that by Saturday morning, March 13, his brigade could be at the Brandenburg Gate. This then was the decision reached. Lüttwitz gave the order for the march on Berlin. Ehrhardt made ready.

Only now did Lüttwitz draw into the plot the group of conspirators of the 'National Union' – Kapp, Pabst, Ludendorff and their associates. They were to stand by to take over the Government in Berlin on Saturday morning. This request, made at such short notice, caught them unprepared. Their own plans for a coup were not yet ready, in large sectors of the country the preparatory organization was not yet completed, no list of ministers had been compiled. But since Lüttwitz and Ehrhardt had fixed a date for the coup, Kapp and his men submitted. The more so as they, too, now felt time to be pressing, for on that day orders were issued for their arrest. These orders were not executed: instead of arresting the conspirators, the Berlin Police had them tipped off. The Police were as 'solidly national' as the *Reichswehr*.

On the following day, Friday, March 12, Berlin was buzzing with rumours. The Berlin evening newspapers even carried news of an imminent coup by the Ehrhardt Brigade. But Noske was not yet ready to take this seriously – at least that was the impression he later gave; and it must be admitted that in the previous nine months there had been more than one coup planned which came to nothing, and rumours of coups which had faded into thin air. Nevertheless Noske took precautions: he summoned two regiments of police and a *Reichswehr* regiment into the government district, for its armed defence in case of need. In this way he thought he had provided for all eventualities. He was about to have the shock of his life.

For on that very evening all the officers of these three regiments agreed to disregard the order to defend the government district. They arranged with the leaders of the remaining units stationed in and around Berlin that none of them would obey a similar order, and for safety's sake got the approval of Seeckt, who held no direct power of command but as Chief of the General Staff naturally enjoyed an impressive degree of military authority. He gave his approval by saying that it was of course out of the question 'to hold manœuvres between Berlin and Potsdam with live ammunition'. Legend has turned this flippant statement (one seems actually to be able to hear the nasal clubman's drawl) into the pithy '*Reichswehr* does not fire on *Reichswehr*'.

In fact *Reichswehr* was perfectly willing to fire on *Reichswehr*. For that evening at 10 p.m. Captain Ehrhardt ordered his brigade 'to march on Berlin in battle order, *to crush any resistance ruthlessly* and to occupy the city centre with its ministries'. Before their arrival in Berlin he drummed it into his troops once again: 'If there is fighting with troops in the government district, you are to act with the utmost severity.' The insurrectionist section of the *Reichswehr* was thus fully prepared to fire on *Reichswehr*; only those *Reichswehr* units which were to oppose the insurrection were not. One part of the *Reichswehr* was resolved to overthrow the Government by force; the other, not to come to its defence. Both acts amounted to mutiny. During this night of March 12 to 13, 1920 Ebert and Noske found themselves abandoned by their armed forces – just as Kaiser Wilhelm II had done on November 9, 1918.

It was an eventful night. From 10 p.m. onwards the Ehrhardt Brigade was marching towards Berlin, in full battle trim, assault packs on their backs, hand-grenades in their belts, as if invading hostile territory. One hour later the Brigade's approach was made known to the Group Command in Berlin. Noske was informed by telephone. Two of the Command's generals, von Oven and von Oldershausen, drove off towards the Brigade allegedly (according to their subsequent testimony after the failure of the coup) to make a last-minute attempt to dissuade Ehrhardt from his plan; in truth probably in order to make a last effort at conciliation between him and Noske. After some difficulty they came face to face with Ehrhardt and persuaded him to give the Government a chance to capitulate before he arrested its members. They had until 7 a.m. to accept Lüttwitz's demands; until then he and his troops would take up positions by the Siegessäule, the victory column. Both generals again telephoned Noske who in his turn called Ebert shortly after midnight and informed him of the ultimatum. Ebert called a Cabinet meeting in the Reich Chancellery for four o'clock in the morning, Noske summoned his commanders to the Reich Defence Ministry at 1 a.m.

At his meeting with the commanders Noske called for their help in the defence of the ministries: he asked in vain. All the generals and staff officers present, with two exceptions, refused to take orders to shoot from the Government. Von Oven and von Oldershausen recommended negotiation with Ehrhardt. Others made excuses: the men would not understand an order to fight, or they were no match for Ehrhardt's Brigade. General Seeckt lectured about comradeship and argued that at any rate it was preferable that Ehrhardt should encounter an uncommitted *Reichswehr* than that he should enter Berlin 'as victor of a successful battle by the Brandenburg Gate'. Embittered, Noske summed up: 'Evidently you do not want to fight.' When no one contradicted him, he cried out: 'Am I then quite abandoned?' The officers remained silent. A broken man, Noske left the Bendlerstrasse at 4 a.m. for the Chancellery, to inform the Cabinet that they were without protection. To his ADC he spoke of suicide.

The nocturnal Cabinet meeting was chaotic. Everyone talked at random and shouted at everyone else; Ebert, in the chair, made a vain attempt to get a more or less orderly discussion going. And yet this panic meeting produced two important results: one was the decision to flee from Berlin; the other a call for a general strike.

Neither decision was taken unanimously. The rift between the Social Democrats and their bourgeois partners in the coalition, long in the offing, broke wide open that night, although in the excitement and confusion of the moment it remained unarticulated. Vice-Chancellor Schiffer, of the Democratic party, and some of the bourgeois ministers did not take part in Ebert's and the Government's flight. They did not want to make a complete break with the mutineers. More important still: the call for the general strike bore only the signature of Ebert and of the Social Democrat ministers. The bourgeois ministers held aloof.

Indeed this call was strong medicine; even for the Social Democrats it meant an unprecedented *volte-face*. In their desperation they had suddenly rediscovered the language of that revolution which a year earlier they had bloodily liquidated with the very troops who now threatened their own safety:

Workers! Comrades! We did not make the Revolution in order to submit now to a régime of bloody mercenaries. We made no pact with the *Baltikum* criminals . . . Everything is at stake. Extreme measures of defence are called for . . . Down tools! Strike! Cut the ground from under the feet of this reactionary clique! Fight with all means for the maintenance of the Republic! Shelve all disputes! There is only one weapon against the dictatorship of Wilhelm II: to paralyse the entire economy! Don't lift a finger! No proletarian must help the military dictatorship! A general strike all along the line! Proletarians, unite! Down with the Counter-Revolution!

The proclamation, decided on by the Social Democrat ministers without the agreement of their bourgeois colleagues, was drafted during the meeting by the Government's chief press officer who put Ebert's and the Social Democrat ministers' names at the bottom in pencil. Only the Reich Chancellor, Bauer, signed with his own hand, the others did not have time to do so: at 6.15 a.m. the meeting was broken off and the ministers jumped into their waiting cars – just ten minutes before Ehrhardt's columns, raucously chanting, marched through the Brandenburg Gate where they were greeted by a group of men in uniform and civilians in 'cutaways' and top hats: Lüttwitz, Ludendorff, Kapp and their followers. When Kapp and his men took over the Chancellery to proclaim the formation of a new government of 'order, liberty and action', they found the chairs still warm.

*

For one whole day, Saturday, March 13, 1920, the *coup d'état* appeared to have been successful. There was no sign of military resistance anywhere. The Berlin garrison as well as the police, the entire Navy, the Army commands in East Prussia, Pomerania, Brandenburg and Silesia formally accepted the authority of the new self-styled Commander-in-Chief Lüttwitz and his Reich Chancellor, Kapp. The Bavarian *Reichswehr* used the opportunity to overthrow, of its own accord, the Social Democrat provincial Government in Munich and to instal a new provincial Government – the notorious Kahr Government under which Hitler rose to strength and which clung to office until that second coup of November 1923 which was already Hitler's work. Elsewhere in Germany the regional army commanders declared neither for nor against Kapp and Lüttwitz; but theirs was not a genuine neutrality: they were merely awaiting the outcome of events. At heart their sympathies were all with the 'new government' and many local commanders made no secret of it. The attitude of the higher-ranking civil servants was not much different: outwardly they appeared to be playing at wait-and-see, inwardly, for the most part, they were in sympathy. Later the allegation was made that Kapp and Lüttwitz foundered for lack of support from the ministerial bureaucracy. It merits no rebuttal. Both the civilian and the military apparatus of state (apart from the Eastern provinces which followed Kapp and Lüttwitz to a man) at best manifested a few signs of cautious hesitation, but they were at all times completely willing 'to do their duty' as ever under the 'new Government' if events should favour it.

The old Government was meanwhile leading a precarious refugee existence. It was no longer in a position to govern: the fugitive ministers no longer had any means of organization – they did not even have typists; they were left only with their lives. They had at first gone to Dresden where General Maercker, Noske's old 'conqueror of the cities', was in command. They hoped to find asylum with him. But Maercker had received telegraphic orders from Berlin on Saturday morning to take the ministers into 'protective custody' when they arrived, and seemed perfectly ready to execute this order, being just polite enough to explain to his superiors that he was really only arresting them for their own protection. It was not the ministers but the leader of the right-wing German Popular Party, Heinze, by chance in Dresden, who initially succeeded in dissuading him from this intention. Later in the day, having indignantly read the Social Democrat call for a general strike, Maercker turned up again to arrest the Government, this time in real earnest. The ministers had to protest at length that their names had been put to this 'draft' without their consent before he would once again change his mind. Ebert and Noske then preferred not to risk a third encounter. After their second adventure with Maercker, the 'old government' chose to continue their flight. That very evening they went on to Stuttgart where the Army had so far remained calm. But it was a matter of several days before the local commander there officially declared his loyalty to the legal government. He did this only after the general strike had done its work and Kapp's and Lüttwitz's position had become untenable.

The general strike began full blast in Berlin on Sunday, March 14, spread to the entire Reich on Monday and promptly completely paralysed the insurgents' Government. It was the most massive strike Germany has ever experienced. The entire country ground to a halt. There were no trains, no trams in the cities, no postal deliveries, no newspapers. All factories were closed. The public administration flagged: the lower officials were on strike, the higher ones found themselves unable to do any effective work in their offices. In Berlin even water, gas and electricity were cut off. People stood in long queues at old-fashioned fountains and wells for drinking water. By the second day of its existence the self-styled government in Berlin had lost all possibility of governing. All communications between capital and provinces were cut. In Berlin itself the military and the administration rapidly lost control over the inhabitants. The 'new government's' tendons and vocal cords had been severed; the machinery of state was free-wheeling.

The only communication with regional army headquarters was by courier and messenger. In vain Kapp and his collaborators drafted conciliatory appeals for a resumption of work, in vain they promised new elections, in vain they decreed the death penalty for strike leaders, in vain they retracted this decree. Nothing of all this got any further than the government district of Berlin. After three days of general strike the *Putsch* government in Berlin had become as impotent as the government in exile in Stuttgart. For both, their writ ran no further than their front doors.

In this week of general strike, from March 14 to 21, 1920, the German proletariat once again repeated its achievement of the week of revolution from November 4 to 10, 1918. The two great events are extraordinarily similar. As on that previous occasion – without central planning or leadership but apparently born of a spontaneous solidarity of thought and feeling – the whole country acted in the same way. As previously, the nature of this mass action was not socialist, but democratic and anti-militarist: as then the Revolution, so now the general strike, was aimed against a military government and thought of as coming to the aid of a civilian government against the military. As previously, the bulk of the strikers consisted of Social Democrats. After all, only the Social Democrat ministers had issued the strike call. The Independents at first refused to join in the call for the strike. ('The SPD has treated us like dogs,' one of their spokesmen, Crispien, told the Berlin trade union leaders on March 13. 'They cannot now ask us to forget everything.') The headquarters of the Berlin KPD, then led by Ernst Reuter who was later to be Mayor of West Berlin during the blockade even issued a call that very day *against* the strike: 'Don't lift a finger for the Government of the murderers of Karl Liebknecht and Rosa Luxemburg, now ignominiously overthrown!' None of this had the slightest effect: the USPD and KPD members, too, went out on strike to a man, and in the end the party leaders had no choice but to join their members. Now was the moment of truth; the counter-Revolution stood unmasked, the SPD had found again the language of revolution, and for the working masses nothing of what had happened since November 9 seemed any longer to count. The hour of socialist unity appeared once more to have struck. In this, too, in taking the reunification of the socialist parties for granted, the mass rising of March 1920 resembled that of November 1918.

In Saxony, Thuringia and above all in the Ruhr area the strike turned into armed revolution in the course of the week. It was triggered off by local *Reichswehr* commanders who made 'common cause with the new government', flew black, white and red flags from barracks and arrested strike pickets. They met resistance; local shooting developed into skirmishes and street battles of varying degrees of violence. The civil war of spring 1919 flared up again, and this time the opponents were differently matched. Then the *Freikorps* had embodied the power of government, now they represented insurrection; then the fighting workers had often been divided and unsure, now this was truer of their military adversaries; then the fighting workers had been on their own in whatever part of the country the conflict reached, now they found backing in the general strike throughout the land; above all, they were now fighting with much more embittered resolution, resentment and desperation than a year before. They had meanwhile come to know the white terror, they knew what to expect if they were defeated. The Revolution which in March 1920 'rose clanking to its feet again' and once again took up the lost battle was no longer as good-natured as it had been in the triumphal mood of November 1918.

In Saxony and Thuringia the military nevertheless ultimately kept the upper hand after the ups and downs of bloody engagements. But in the Ruhr area a military miracle occurred. After the first victorious skirmishes an improvised Red Army thundered across the region like an avalanche. On March 17 it took Dortmund, on the 18th Hamm and Bochum, on the 19th Essen. Whereupon the regional command in Münster ordered the demoralized garrisons to withdraw also from Düsseldorf, Mülheim, Duisburg, Hamborn and Dinslaken. By the end of the strike week the whole of the Ruhr area was under the control of the armed workers.

It was this unexpected display of strength by the renascent revolution which was also to be its downfall. The general strike had made the Kapp government untenable, on this its military backers were soon agreed. But fear of the Revolution, which seemed suddenly to be surging to life again just when its defeat had seemed final, within a few days restored unity among the opponents of March 13. Confronted by the Revolution, bourgeois state and military rebels quickly made common cause again. And it was not long before the SPD, too, veered to join this united front and betrayed the Revolution for a second time.

On March 13 Kapp had taken Vice-Chancellor Schiffer, who had stayed in Berlin, into protective custody, along with the ministers of the Prussian State Government. On the very next day – the general strike had begun – they were again free and one day later negotiations were in full swing. The leaders of the two right-wing bourgeois parties, Oskar Hergt and Stresemann, intervened in these negotiations which showed the four bourgeois parties to be instinctively allied. All four were agreed that the main danger now was 'Bolshevism' and the main task was to 'win back' the officers' corps. Vice-Chancellor Schiffer spoke everybody's mind when he said it was not desirable for Kapp and Lüttwitz to be overthrown by a 'mutiny' of their troops or a general strike; both would lead to 'Bolshevism'. They would have to be persuaded to resign; they would have to be offered an easy way out. As early as this a tacit coalition of the four bourgeois parties began to take shape – the coalition of the bourgeois block which a few months later was to take over the government of the Weimar Republic and to hold it, with brief interruptions, until its dissolution. The compromise with the military rebels, which finally settled the Kapp coup without victors and vanquished, was its first political action.

In return for Kapp and Lüttwitz's voluntary resignation, the four parties, with the consent of a handful of Social Democrat politicians still in Berlin, offered new elections, a reconstruction of the Cabinet and an amnesty for all participants in the coup. The rebels played poker. At first they only withdrew Kapp who in their eyes had in any case shown himself to be a dud. Lüttwitz endeavoured to remain military dictator for another day. But then, somewhat like Noske on an earlier occasion, he saw himself abandoned by his military commanders. They, too, now felt that it was time to reconstitute a united front against 'Bolshevism'. To Vice-Chancellor Schiffer who was now conducting the government's business in Berlin – nominally still in the name of the Weimar coalition, in reality already with the support of the four bourgeois parties – they proposed General von Seeckt as Commander-in-Chief of the *Reichswehr* and Schiffer, acting in Ebert's name though without his knowledge, appointed him.

The negotiations had been conducted throughout in the friendliest terms. The chief negotiator for the rebels was Captain Pabst, the murderer of Liebknecht and Rosa Luxemburg, who as recently as March 13 had been promoted Major by Lüttwitz (the promotion was never rescinded). When he called on Schiffer on the evening of March 16 to begin the negotiations, he was first offered a splendid supper. The Vice-Chancellor later noted: 'This at least produced an atmosphere which, if inappropriate to the seriousness of the situation, at least had no unfavourable effect on it.' When two days later Pabst brought him Lüttwitz's resignation – which the Vice-Chancellor accepted at once in the name of the Reich President, agreeing at the same time to the pension provisions it contained – Schiffer pressed Pabst to stay out of harm's way until the National Assembly had settled the amnesty issue and to offer the same advice to Lüttwitz. 'Schiffer even offered false passports and money for both of them, which Pabst declined with thanks. The insurrectionists had already procured false passports from their friends at Police Headquarters', writes Johannes Erger, in his new and detailed study *Der Kapp-Lüttwitz-Putsch*, basing his words on corroborating statements by the two protagonists.

Ehrhardt received even better treatment than Pabst and Lüttwitz. The new Chief of the *Reichswehr*, Seeckt, 'in an order of the day of 18.3., after a meeting with Ehrhardt, commended the discipline of the Brigade, recognized that they had acted in the belief that they were "serving the interests of the Fatherland" and on 19.3. assured Ehrhardt in writing that he would be safe from arrest as long as he was in command of the Brigade' (Erger). Only then did the Brigade march out of Berlin – singing and with flags flying, as they had marched in. When they met with booing from a hostile crowd at the Brandenburg Gate, they unhesitatingly fired with machine-guns into the crowd. It was their parting shot. Twelve dead and thirty seriously injured were left lying on the cobblestones of the Pariser Platz.

The Reich Government was now able to return to Berlin from Stuttgart. Its first concern was to end the general strike which was still continuing, its second to disarm the Red Army which still occupied the Ruhr area. Unprompted, the Social Democrat ministers, who in its moment of need had once again called on the Revolution to help and had indeed been rescued by it, found their way back into their familiar role as the fig-leaf of the counter-Revolution. To the union leaders who were reluctant to call off the strike, they made promises they knew they *could not* keep, such as stiff penalties against the participants in the coup; or promises they had *no intention* of keeping, such as the drafting of workers into the security forces. The Red Army in the Ruhr got a short-term ultimatum to lay down its arms. Then the matter was entrusted to the *Reichswehr* which 'had returned to a constitutional basis'. The *Reichswehr* deliberately used for this purpose chiefly those units which had taken part in the rising against the Government under Kapp and Lüttwitz; *inter alia* the *Freikorps* Epp, Pfeffer, Lützow, Lichtschlag and Rossbach as well as the Marine Brigade Löwenfeldt, a sister unit to Ehrhardt's Brigade. They were now to have a chance to show their mettle once again. How they set about it is testified to in a letter from a member of the Epp Brigade:

To the Reserve Field Hospital I, Station 9,
Wischerhöfen, 2 April '20

Dear Nurses and Patients,

Am now at last with my company. Yesterday morning I got to my company and at 1 p.m. we made the first assault. If I were to write you everything, you would say these are lies. No mercy is shown. We shoot even the wounded. The enthusiasm is marvellous, almost incredible. Our battalion has two dead, the reds 200 to 300. Anyone who falls into our hands gets first the gun butt and then the bullet. During the entire action I thought of station A. That is due to the fact that we also shot dead instantly ten red-cross nurses each of whom was carrying a pistol. We shot at these abominations with joy, and how they cried and pleaded with us for their lives! Nothing doing! Whoever is found carrying arms is our enemy and gets done. We were much more humane against the French in the field. How are things in the hospital? The population gives us everything. In the pubs we often get free drinks, 20 to 30 of us. My address is: Oberjäger Max Ziller, Student, 11 Kompanie, Brigade Epp, Post Rokow in Westfalen.

So ended the Kapp Putsch: with a murderously punitive expedition by the Government, still headed by Social Democrats, against its saviours, mounted by those from whom it had been saved.

But the SPD now had to face the judgement of its adherents. The new elections promised to the insurrectionists could no longer be postponed. In April the National Assembly was dissolved, on June 6 a new Reichstag elected. In this election the SPD paid for its great betrayal of the Revolution, of which it had given such impressive evidence once more after the Kapp coup. At one blow it lost more than half its supporters.

In January 1919 12½ million voters had voted SPD. Now there were only 5½ million. And the collapse of the SPD deprived the Weimar coalition of its Parliamentary majority – for good. There began that epoch of bourgeois block governments which lasted to the end of the Weimar Republic and was resumed after the foundation of the Bonn Federal Republic.

For half a century the SPD had waited for its hour to come. It had come and gone. Another half-century had to pass before it came again.

> Reject the minute's gift – and all eternity
> will not renew the offer.

15. Three Legends

There can hardly be any event in history about which so many lies have been told as the German Revolution of 1918. Three legends in particular have proved hardy perennials.

The first one is particularly widespread – even today – among the German bourgeoisie. It quite simply denies the Revolution. No real revolution, one is still frequently told, took place in Germany in 1918. All that happened was a collapse. It was merely the momentary weakness of the powers of law and order in the wake of defeat which allowed a sailors' mutiny to seem like a revolution.

How wrong and blind this is becomes immediately evident when one compares 1918 with 1945. Then, indeed, there was merely a collapse.

Admittedly, a sailors' mutiny in 1918 sparked off the Revolution, but it was only the spark. The extraordinary fact remains: a mere sailors' mutiny in the first week of November 1918 set off an earthquake which shook all Germany; the entire home army, the entire urban working class, in Bavaria in addition a section of the rural population joined in the rising. This rising was no longer a mere mutiny, it was a genuine revolution. It was no longer, as it had been on October 29 and 30 with the High Seas Fleet at Schillig-Reede, a matter of disobeying orders. It was a matter of overthrowing a ruling class and changing the structure of a state. And what is a revolution if not just that?

Like every revolution this one overthrew an old order and replaced it with the beginnings of a new one. It was not merely destructive, it was also creative. Its creation was the Workers' and Soldiers' Councils. If everything did not go smoothly and tidily, if the new order did not at once function as competently as the old one, if regrettable and ludicrous elements were present – of what revolution would this not have been true? And that the Revolution broke out at a moment of weakness and fear in the old order and owed its victory in part to this weakness, is equally self-evident. The same is true of any other revolution in history.

Against this, the German Revolution of November 1918 deserves special praise for its self-discipline, mildness and humanity which are all the more remarkable in that the Revolution was almost everywhere the spontaneous work of leaderless masses. The masses were the real heroes of this Revolution and it is more than chance that German theatre and film of those years reached their apogee with grandiose mass scenes, and that Ernst Toller's then famous revolutionary drama was called *Masse Mensch* (the human mass). As a revolutionary achievement by the masses, November 1918 in Germany is on a par with July 1789 in France and March 1917 in Russia.

There is one final piece of evidence to prove that the German Revolution was no hallucination, no spectre, but a reality of flesh and bone: those rivers of blood that were shed in the first half of 1919 to 'roll back' and crush the Revolution.

There is no doubt about who crushed the Revolution. It was the SPD leadership, it was Ebert and his men. There is also no doubt that, in order to be able to crush the Revolution, the SPD leaders at first placed themselves at its head, that thus they betrayed it. In the words of that impartial and expert witness Ernst Troeltsch, the SPD leaders 'for the sake of its effect on the masses adopted as their own long-promised child the Revolution which they had not made and which from their point of view was a miscarriage'.

This is a moment for exactitude: every word counts. It is correct to say that the SPD leaders had not made the Revolution and had not wanted it. But it is inaccurate to say that they merely 'adopted' it. They had not merely adopted the Revolution, it was indeed their own, long-promised, child. For fifty years they had preached and promised it. Even if now 'their own, long-promised child' had now become for the SPD an unwanted child, the SPD was and remained its real mother, and if she killed it, it was infanticide.

Any infanticidal mother might plead a stillborn or miscarried child. The SPD did likewise. That is the origin of the second great legend about the German Revolution: that it was not the revolution which the Social Democrats had been proclaiming for fifty years, but a Bolshevist revolution, something imported from Russia, and that the SPD had protected and saved Germany from 'Bolshevist chaos' (the expression 'Bolshevist chaos' is in itself a terminological lie; Bolshevism, whatever may be said against it, is the very opposite of chaos, namely the most rigid, dictatorial, even tyrannical, order).

This legend, invented by the Social Democrats, is supported by the Communists, intentionally or not, for they claim the entire merit of the Revolution for the KPD or for its predecessor, the Spartacist Union, and thus vaingloriously confirm what the Social Democrats plead in self-justification: that the Revolution of 1918 was a Communist (or 'Bolshevik') revolution.

But even if Social Democrats and Communists for once say the same thing, that does not make it true. The Revolution of 1918 was not imported from Russia. It was home-grown German produce. And it was not a Communist, but a Social Democrat revolution – the very revolution which the SPD had prophesied and demanded for fifty years, and for which it had prepared its millions of supporters. It was as the instrument of this revolution that the Party posed throughout.

This is easy to prove. It was not the Spartacist Union with its inadequate numbers and organization which made the Revolution, but millions of Social Democrat voting workers and soldiers. The government demanded by these millions – in January 1919 as much as in November 1918 – was no Spartacist or Communist government, but a government of the reunited Social Democrat party. The constitution they were striving for was no dictatorship of the proletariat, but a proletarian democracy. The proletariat was to replace the bourgeoisie as ruling class, but it aimed to rule democratically, not dictatorially. Stripped of their power, the former ruling classes and their parties were to remain free to join in Parliamentary discussion, roughly in the way in which the Social Democrats had been free to in the Kaiser's Empire.

The methods of the Revolution, too – perhaps to its disadvantage – were anything but Bolshevist or Leninist. At a closer look, they were not even Marxist, but rather in the style of Lassalle: the decisive lever of power, for which the revolutionary workers, sailors and soldiers reached out, was not ownership of the means of production, as Marxist teaching would have indicated, but the power of government. In this sense, as the Social Democrat battle song had it, they entered upon

> the road along which Lassalle led us.

As the Social Democrat pioneer Ferdinand Lassalle – not Marx – had demanded in the 1860s, the revolutionary masses aimed at seizing administrative rather than economic power. It was not factories they occupied, but public offices and barracks. As 'People's Commissars' they elected the Social Democrat leaders.

And these leaders, once they had accepted the power of government from the Revolution, used it for the bloody repression of that Revolution – their own long-promised, at last realized, Revolution. They pointed cannon and machine-guns at their own supporters. What the Kaiser had in vain tried to do – to unleash the returning field armies upon the revolutionary workers – Ebert likewise tried to do from the very outset. And when he likewise failed, he did not hesitate to take the further step of arming and mobilizing against his unsuspecting supporters the most extreme adherents of counter-Revolution, the enemies even of bourgeois democracy, indeed his own enemies, the predecessors of Fascism in Germany.

These are the facts: the Revolution which was bloodily crushed by the SPD and from which, if you like, it 'preserved' or 'saved' Germany, was no Communist revolution but a Social Democrat one. The Social Democrat revolution which took place in Germany in 1918 was – as Prince Max von Baden had prophetically hoped during the week before November 9 – 'stifled' – stifled in its own blood, not by the princes and monarchs it had overthrown, but by its own leaders whom it had trustingly carried to power. It was crushed with extreme and ruthless violence, not in honest battle, but from the back, through betrayal.

No matter what side one is on and whether one welcomes or deplores the outcome, this betrayal has earned for Ebert and Noske an inglorious immortality. Two judgements still echo down the corridors of history which were uttered in those days and counter-signed by the speakers with their lives. Franz Mehring, Social Democrat party veteran and party historian, said in January 1919, shortly before he died of a broken heart: 'No Government has ever sunk lower.' And Gustav Landauer, not long before he died at the hands – or more precisely, under the boots – of Noske's *Freikorps* soldiers, said: 'In the entire realm of natural history I know of no creature more repulsive than the Social Democrat Party.'

Ebert and Noske were not evil-doers on an epic scale like Hitler, they were commonplace – devastatingly so. The monstrosity of their actions in history is not reflected in their personal characters. The enquiry into their motives reveals nothing daemonic, no grandly satanic elements, only the trivial impulses of the petty-bourgeois pedant and social climber. One can accept without hesitation that they sincerely detested and had an almost panic-stricken fear of the disorder which attaches to every revolution, even if curiously enough they showed no such fear of the equally great – and bloodier – disorder of the counter-Revolution. More deep seated even was the vanity of the little man who is suddenly admitted to society and, what is more, called to its rescue. When bourgeois colleagues in Parliament treated the former 'unpatriotic scum' with sudden respect, when men like Groener and Prince Max accorded them flattering familiarity, when even the Kaiser and Hindenburg manifested gracious condescension, when in their hour of need all these feared and envied people acknowledged Ebert and his men to be their last remaining life-belt – a warm wave of proud and grateful loyalty swept over the recipients of such honours and they were ready to make any sacrifice, even human sacrifices by the thousand. They readily sacrificed those who followed and trusted them to those who were now patroniz-ing them. The unspeakable was perpetrated with stout hearts and loyally uplifted eyes.

When the generals, princes and Grande Bourgeoisie 'entrusted the German Empire to Ebert's care', he trusted them as unsuspect-ingly as he was trusted by the Social Democrat workers, sailors and soldiers who made the Revolution. And as he betrayed the Revolution, so those whom his treason served betrayed him, once his work was done. The means they used was the third of the three great legends about the German Revolution – the legend of the stab in the back.

The claim that the Social Democrat Revolution was to blame for Germany's defeat and had 'stabbed the victorious front in the back' was publicly made by Hindenburg and Ludendorff as soon as Ebert and Noske had completed the subdual of the Revolution, and the Germans obediently believed it for a quarter of a century.

This claim was itself a stab in the back – into the back of the Social Democrat leaders whom, in October and November 1918, Imperial Germany had summoned to shoulder her defeat and undertake her rescue. (Ludendorff: 'Let them now cope with the mess . . .')

After they had loyally shouldered the burden of defeat (Ebert to the returning troops: 'No enemy has vanquished you') and had brought the corpse of the revolution to drop it, retriever-fashion, at the feet of the German bourgeoisie, they got their reward in the shape of the legend of the stab in the back. Ebert himself was literally hunted to death in the ensuing years with the completely unfounded, but incessantly repeated and judicially approved reproach of 'High Treason'.

One might feel sorry for him if there were not a kind of ironical justice in the way history took its revenge on him. There is a ballad by the German poetess Annette von Droste-Hülshoff which provides an exact analogy for Ebert's fate.

During a shipwreck someone murders a fellow passenger by pushing him off the plank to which he clings. By chance the manufacturer's stamp on the plank stays in his memory: 'Batavia 510.' The murder is never discovered. But when the murderer reaches dry land, he is mistaken for a long-sought pirate, sentenced to death and led to his execution.

> And as in his derision's pride
> He looks up at the sky again
> This on the gallows he espied:
> 'Batavia 510'.

The poem is called *Retaliation*.

In exactly the same roundabout, but neat, fashion, retaliation struck at Ebert for what he had done to the Revolution. He was hunted to death with a lie, with the reproach of a treason he had never committed. But this reproach could never have touched him if it had not been for the other treason he did in fact commit. He had stabbed in the back, not the victorious front, but the victorious revolution. For the sake of those who were now stabbing him in the back – with the lie of the stab in the back.

It is difficult to suppress a certain satisfaction at the aesthetic perfection of this complicated symmetry. It is as if at the climax of a symphonic composition all themes meet – and disclose their common root. On the surface the lie about the stab in the back bitterly wronged Ebert. At a deeper level, he got his deserts. He was betrayed as he had betrayed, and he could only be betrayed *because* he had betrayed.

On September 29, 1918 Ludendorff shifted the burden of his defeat on to the Social Democrats in order to be able later to 'frame them'. The Revolution came to their aid; it was about to smash the trap he had set for them and in which they were unknowingly caught. But they betrayed the Revolution – and the trap snapped shut. There, in three sentences, is the entire story. A terrible story, but not a meaningless one. It might be entitled: 'The punishment fits the crime.'

Alas, the punishment for the great betrayal of the German Revolution of 1918 hit not only those who deserved it.

The collective hero of the Revolution, the German working class, never recovered from the blow. Socialist unity, for which they had fought and bled so bravely, was lost for ever in 1918. From that great betrayal dates the great schism of Socialism and the inextinguishable hatred between Communists and Social Democrats – a hatred as between wolves and dogs. (A dog, of course, was once a wolf, domesticated by man for his own purposes. The Social Democrats were once a workers' party, domesticated by capitalism for its own purposes.) The same workers who in 1918 – and again in 1919 and 1920 – fought so courageously and lucklessly, found their fighting spirit broken when fifteen years later they would have needed it again – against

Hitler. Their sons of 1945 were no longer able to repeat their fathers' prowess of 1918. Their grandchildren of today no longer even know of it. The German workers' revolutionary tradition is extinguished.

But the German people as a whole, including those of its bourgeois classes who welcomed the failure of the Revolution with understandable relief and delight, had to pay a heavy price for that failure: the Third Reich, the renewed World War, the second and more overwhelming defeat and the loss of their national unity and sovereignty. The seed for all this was already to be found in the counter-Revolution triggered off by the Social Democrat leaders. A victorious German Revolution might have saved Germany from it all.

Even today there are many 'Ebert Germans' who hate every revolution 'like sin'; even today there are many who disown the Revolution of 1918 as if it were a blot on the national escutcheon. But the Revolution is no disgrace. Coming after four years of starvation and exhaustion, it was something to be proud of. The disgrace was its betrayal.

Of course revolutions are not made for fun; of course it is part of statesmanship to prevent revolutions by timely reforms. Every revolution is a painful, bloody and terrible process – like a birth. But like every birth, every successful revolution is at the same time a creative, life-giving process.

All those nations who have gone through a great revolution look back on it with pride; and every victorious revolution has for a time thrust greatness upon the people who made it: Holland and England in the seventeenth century as much as America and France in the eighteenth and nineteenth, and Russia and China in the twentieth. It is not the victorious revolutions that cripple a nation, it is the ones that are stifled and suppressed, betrayed and disowned.

To this day Germany is crippled by the betrayal of 1918.

Index of Persons

Please remember that this is a library book, and that it belongs only temporarily to each person who uses it. Be considerate. Do not write in this, or any, library book.

DATE DUE

DEMCO 38-296